FOUNDER FUNDAMENTALS

THE GROWING ENTREPRENEUR'S
4 STEP GUIDE
TO BUILDING AND LEADING
A HIGH PERFORMANCE DREAM TEAM

BRETT HILKER

ISBN: 978-1-7770643-1-0 (ebook)

ISBN: 978-1-7770643-0-3 (paperback)

Cover design by: *100Covers.com*
Interior formatting by: *FormattedBooks.com*

DEDICATION

I dedicate this book to:

Mom, Dad, and Krysta for your constant love and support. I wouldn't be where I am today without you.

My College Pro family for opening up the path that has provided me so many cherished relationships and an arena to develop my own fundamentals as an entrepreneur.

My SPS family for your guidance, expertise, and encouragement in making this book a reality.

My readers! This book is, and always will be, for you!

CONTENTS

SQUEEZING THE MOST OUT OF THESE PAGES

Treat this book like a tool and a resource.

Mark it up, highlight, fold the pages, and write in the margins. Trust me, it can take it.

Bring it with you and refer back to it.

Do whatever it takes for these fundamentals to stick: no judgements here.

Perfectly polished books on shelves never helped anyone.

INTRODUCTION

You're excited to be building your vision, but after weeks and months of grinding hard, everyone you hire keeps quitting.

You're bending over backwards to make your handful of customers happy, and yet you are constantly running around in circles fixing problems.

Your happiness exists within the cracks of your schedule: The tiny calms between exhausting storms. And just when you think you have found a hint of stability, you are bombarded with a cascading inbox and a chiming phone that could vibrate off a table.

More demands on your time. Long days, late nights, and seemingly earlier and earlier mornings.

It feels like every time you try and move forward, you step on a landmine full of new problems.

You lie awake thinking about the successful founders you see online, on bookshelves, and in documentaries:

"What do they have that I don't?"

"What is the special sauce that made them successful?"

"What made people want to follow them?"

This is the all too common reality of entrepreneurship for the majority of people who start out making their best attempt at building their business dreams. The ambition and vision are there, but the know-how isn't. This blind excitement quickly turns into overwhelm and confusion. As Elon Musk says, "Starting a company is like eating glass and staring into the abyss." No wonder most people quit. Entrepreneurship can be unpredictable pain and constant disappointment!

But it doesn't have to be this way.

It doesn't have to be this painful and exhausting, if you let me show you how.

This book is for the budding entrepreneur who is just getting going.

It is for those that have got a bit of traction and want to grow by working smarter.

It's also for those that have a lot of traction, but at the expense of almost everything.

This book is NOT for the guy who cashed out and bought a penthouse.

This book is NOT for billionaires or their executive assistants.

If you have it all together, your business is growing like it should, and you're happy, you can stop reading right now. I'll save you the trouble. This book is not for you.

This is the culmination of years of trial and error, massive wins, tragic losses, and all the unshakable systems I've learned from those before me that have been battle-tested for decades. These are the strategies that have repeatedly produced successful new founders and sustainable businesses in the thousands.

Skeptical?

Yup. Totally get it.

The pain you're feeling is real. It's hard to believe you can stay afloat the way things are, let alone improve things. It's hard to picture a business that has sustainable momentum. A business that can carry its own weight. But know that this is how millions of budding founders feel right now. This is how millions have felt before you. And, the ones that pushed through and succeeded had some things in common.

As the age-old adage goes, you don't have to reinvent the wheel.

Learn through our pain, our mistakes, and our systems for success. The only thing I ask is for you to be open to them. When I was a young entrepreneur, the biggest transformation I saw that radically shifted the growth I achieved was being coachable. Shifting from the *"I've tried everything"* mindset to the *"I'll try anything"* mindset had virtually immediate positive results.

Now, after millions in sales, dozens of employees, thousands of customers, and coaching hundreds of entrepreneurs, trust me, there are some things that just work.

Founder Fundamentals is broken down into four simple foundations. And after a decade of being in the trenches, running multiple businesses, and coaching a lot of overwhelmed entrepreneurs, I get a lot of common responses:

"Why didn't I learn this in business school?"

"Brett, how did you know that was the issue?"

"I wish I would've known this years ago!"

"Thank you. You saved my business."

By the end of this book, all of your questions will be answered, like:

"Why can't I find good people?"

"Why does everyone quit?"

"How am I ever going to hit my goals?"

"Are these goals even worth it?"

"Why won't people take me seriously?"

"Why can't I escape all these problems?"

I promise this book will reduce your turnover to zero and double your business…

if…

You lean in.

If you engage and squeeze every drop from these pages.

Right now.

Don't let your pride be an anchor.

Don't let your lack of time be an anchor (you really need this book if you don't have this bit of time).

This book will change the course of your business and your life as an entrepreneur.

Every day that goes by means that money is slipping through your fingers, good people are walking away, and the entrepreneurship hamster wheel you are stuck on is slowly wearing you down.

Let's get it done. Your future self and your future dream team will thank you.

SECTION 1
INTERNAL WIRING

CHAPTER 1: INTROSPECTION

Introspection

Humans are amazing and are capable of consistently pulling off seemingly impossible feats. Climbing Mount Everest, running a four-minute mile, and landing on the moon, among countless other examples, were all thought to be unachievable. But, they have all been done. Not only have they been accomplished, but achievements like these lay the foundations to build from for future generations to stretch further.

The foundation of facing challenges and doing hard things needs to begin from within. Starting a business passes what I call the Hard Thing Test with flying colors. It may seem counterintuitive to start with heavy stuff like self-awareness first, but it will lay the foundation and make everything else easier as a result. We need to have some insight into our strengths, style, and capabilities, so we are ready to accept those challenges and do those hard things. A little introspection is a necessary first step.

Introspection first made a grand entrance into my life when I was starting my first company. I had landed clients, set deadlines, and hired staff with contracts and salaries. It didn't take long to realize that this I was in charge and steering this whole ship alone. In my naivete, I had blindly set very lofty expectations for everyone involved, which ultimately came back to bite me pretty hard all in one week.

I started a painting business in the summer to get me through a year of postsecondary expenses. My initial thought was that it would be a pretty straightforward summer; working hard with some friends and painting fences, windows, and doors for homeowners in my community.

The third week in May, however, proved to be a paradigm-shifting moment for me. Past-Brett would have never believed me if I had the opportunity to go back in time and explain it to him. It was a Monday morning, and I was still half asleep as I rolled out of bed to get up and out to the jobsite. I had stayed up late the night before packing up my rusty 1991 Chevy Cavalier station wagon with equipment for a new training week. My pillow seemed to have more gravity than usual.

At this time of year, mornings were usually sunny, but for someone that wasn't fully prepared (like Sleepy Brett that morning), the brisk air felt like an ice bath once I stepped outside. There was a bit of frost on the windows when I creaked open the door and plopped myself onto the tired cushions of the driver's seat.

To no surprise, I could still see my breath once I closed the door, which was met with universal clanking and squeaking from all the equipment behind my head. Everything rattled a little more in the mornings and my car was packed from floor to ceiling. My tired eyes stared over the greasy steering wheel as I pumped the gas pedal to start the engine. I had to get more and more creative every morning with the number and finesse of the pumps to start it. That morning, the magic number was five small pumps and one large one at the end as I turned the key. My $500 car probably felt as tired as I did all the time.

Getting to the site was a blur, but I needed to bring my A game that morning to pump up my crew and give them the "boss" I thought they needed. I wanted them to feel confident about working for me. We were only two days into this job, and I could already see that there was an underlying tension of frustration and anger. Just reading the body language and overhearing some comments made by my crew let me know something was up.

I expected them to be the quick learners they said they were during their interviews. They were expecting this two-day job to be finished after two days, get paid, and move onto the next project like I said during their interviews. Instead, we were still at the same house for a third morning with still more work to do (we're going to discuss expectation setting a little later).

I started the day giving out my version of assertive commands and assigning tasks to each of them. I felt like I was directing rush hour traffic in the middle of a busy intersection. In the moment, it felt productive, as if the tone I was using would make up for their lack of experience and they would just "get it." They were moving equipment around, asking questions, and making a game plan to be efficient. To an outside eye, they were on task and working hard. But moving forward in the right direction and plain old movement are two different things that feel the exact same way when you start anything new. You don't know what you don't know. We were going through the motions in real time, but not making forward progress. I just didn't know it yet.

Being busy meant being productive at this stage of my business and I needed to go do a bank deposit some time that day. So, once I got them moving, I told them I'd be back in thirty minutes.

"It's not too long."

"They know exactly what to do."

"What could happen?"

These are the thoughts I told myself while pumping the gas pedal twice to start the car. Famous last words.

When I got back, that blind confidence immediately fell apart. In the short time I was away, one painter spilled paint on the sidewalk and then tried to clean it up with a pressure washer so I wouldn't notice. The high-pressure water carved messy childlike cursive scribbles into the sidewalk. His attempt to remove all the purple evidence of his clumsiness from the fresh concrete was unsuccessful to put it nicely.

Another painter changed the color scheme and put that same purple destined for the wood siding onto the white windows of the entire rear of the house. My other painter "finished" his two windows (they were not even close to being done) and was sitting on the grass, killing spiders with a putty knife when I walked through the back gate. I wish I was making that up.

This is where it all fell apart (if it hadn't already). I lost my cool and the argument that ensued was mostly a three versus one battle of me ripping into them for their lack of detail and care, and them ripping into me for not training them well enough and underestimating how long this supposed two-day job was taking.

When the dust settled, they all walked off the jobsite. I was left fuming in anger with equipment scattered everywhere, a house that looked like The Joker, and a client that was going to be home in two hours to set up for her mother's birthday party that night.

I decided to focus on the task at hand and try to fix as much of the damage as possible in the few moments I had before she got home. This may come as no shock, but the damage of three people can't be easily undone quickly with just one person.

Tammy was furious.

Embarrassed by her own home, she kept everyone inside that night so her family wouldn't see the aftermath of our actions earlier that day. I spent the rest of the week doing everything in my power to overdeliver and make her happy. I was sanding walls in the rain, painting all day, calling her with updates, and bending to her every request in the hopes it would cause short-term memory loss and she would forget how the job started.

When we finally did the last inspection, it was Saturday morning, not Tuesday night, like I promised, and she was satisfied. Just satisfied. In her mind, I was barely able to drag her experience across the finish line. She could be in the backyard now and not scoff and what she saw. She would tell her friends about how I saved the project if they asked, but she would never recommend me to them. To make things worse, I only got paid half of what we agreed to in the contract.

Looking back, I overpromised (and completely underdelivered) because I wanted my staff and clients to think I was professional and knew what I was doing. It was a projection and a facade to compensate for my lack of confidence and knowledge. I blindly believed that I could just "figure it out," but that mindset of false confidence ended up being the very thing that knocked my ego down a few rungs on the ladder. This was an opportunity for introspection and I was forever grateful that I took the time to take stock and evaluate my experiences. The long-term gains have far outshined that short-term pain that the week at Tammy's house served me.

We all have that inner voice that asks "What do others think of me?" This is the surface level starting place of a much deeper self-awareness exercise. Not only do we need to address this question itself, but we need to know why we are thinking these thoughts. Not knowing ourselves can lead us down dark roads full of potholes.

As a founder, it's important to develop a healthy relationship between the outer world and our internal one. It isn't unhealthy to think about how others see us or have concerns about how we are perceived and understood in the world. When we take these questions and they are contextualized or filtered through a "Why" question, we can gain a deeper understanding for the people and environments we interact with.

"Why did I react that way?"

"Why do I get stressed when _____ happens?"

The same holds true for processing internal thoughts before we turn them into external actions. Our actions become more objective and beneficial by putting them through the Why Filter first before acting. We gain clarity about the origins of our thoughts and the outcomes of our actions. The more often we use the Why Filter, the stronger our thought processes become, and we get more positive results by using it as an important decision-making tool. Our brains like the reward of positive experiences, so asking why then becomes a habit you don't need to think about as you use it more and more. Just adding this skill to your thought process can create a snowball effect of better outcomes.

The two concepts of introspection and self-awareness are necessary blocks in your foundation. On the surface, they may seem the same, but are actually quite different. Self-awareness is the destination and introspection is the vehicle to get there. Introspection is the process through which we gain self-awareness and there are many tools that can help. Knowing ourselves and being aware of how we act or think is crucial to success.

What is our personality type?

How do we feel about our circumstances?

What are our true motives?

All of these answers give us a better understanding of why we operate like we do and show us where our strengths and weaknesses lie.

This is the foundational mindset to push past comfort zones, chase dreams, and build companies. It's the point where you don't just become mindful of your thoughts, but diagnose them and understand where they came from. It is a skill that takes a lot of training and discipline to keep top of mind. Mastering self-awareness seems to always be one step ahead, since the process sometimes uncovers more interesting questions than meaningful answers.

Now, this is a good problem to have as it means our decision making improves dramatically (although it will never be perfect—I still make some ridiculous decisions) and our results grow. It's a positive feedback loop where self-exploration and self-awareness help you find the answers you are looking for as well as more questions you didn't know you needed to ask. While we will never be perfect, the growth experience gained from increasing your self-awareness moves you from a place of subjective reality to that of one closer to an objective one. Biased to less biased.

Your Lenses

Growing up, I was accustomed to being able to pull things off last minute. I would stay up all night finishing up a school project. Plans with friends were left until the last minute but came together just in time. I would start training for tryouts at the latest possible time in the variety of sports I played. I almost always, with few exceptions, got it done and put out a good performance.

Succeeding enough times with this mindset gave me the lens and viewpoint that I didn't need to prepare. This is exactly why I viewed the situation with my painters and Tammy no differently. I would just figure it out and pull it off "on the fly," as I always did. I was blind to the difference between all those times in school and that hell week of painting mishaps. I didn't take into consideration that I wasn't the only factor involved in the execution of the work.

There is satisfaction in doing everything yourself. You control the final product since your hand is involved, very intimately, with every step of the process. Now, starting a business, I couldn't be in all places at once. I had to rely on transferring the ideas and vision I had to my team and turn those ideas into action through the hands of others.

The lens I placed onto that particular situation was from a version of Past-Brett that wouldn't withstand the demands of his current environment, responsibilities, and goals. Introspection was recognizing that that lens existed.

I needed to get past the negative self-talk—calling myself an idiot, getting angry, or regretful feelings I had for hiring those three painters—and understand the decision-making process that led to those horrendous results. That's the bedrock. The introspective moment was when I began to take my finger-pointing and shift it back toward myself. What were the decisions, small and large, I made that added up to that situation? What did I do, think, and say? That's the starting point.

The amazing thing about how we see the world through these lenses, is that we all have a unique viewpoint. They change or become more fortified as we have more life experiences, are introduced to new environments, and establish relationships with new people. It's the way we all experience the world around us. And I don't mean in a literal sense! Even people that have lost their sight have a lens in which they experience the world.

Your lens on the world of marriage will be colored differently if grew up with parents that were together or divorced.

Your lens on the world of spirituality with be colored differently depending on what faith you were brought up in, if you were brought up with a certain religion.

The sports teams we paint our faces for and the bitter rivals we scream and curse at are choices based on lenses.

The lens through which we view money is a learned habit. Financial decisions in our daily lives are based on how we were trained growing up and who we choose to surround ourselves with.

Our view on other cultures varies dramatically based on how we were raised and the travelling we've done.

Once we understand that every decision we make and every thought we have is based on lenses that were created through our immediate environment, how we were raised, and the people we surround ourselves with, it is easier to be more objective and use our Why Filter to predict the results of those decisions.

As a founder, the awareness of these lenses helps create better decisions and more understanding relationships between your customers and employees. Over time, don't be surprised if this increased awareness begins to shift the lens itself. Then, as more and more decisions turn into results within these interactions inside your business, awareness becomes a useful tool to self-correct if the results aren't the ones we desire.

After that week at Tammy's purple house, I did some serious thinking about how my actions got me to those results. I concluded three things:

1.   I defaulted to my "I will figure it out as I go" mindset that had served me in the past and promised unrealistic results to my painters and Tammy. I was looking through the lens that told me that I would find a way and pull it off somehow like usual.

2.   I hired my employees with the mindset of me not wanting to reject them and be the bad guy for saying "No." I didn't consider the objective factors like cultural fit and skill level. (We'll get into that more in Section 2).

3.   Ultimately, these were things I could control.

Empathy

A by-product of identifying and unpacking these viewpoints for ourselves will at first be discomfort—as strengthening any new muscle will be—but will lead to a greater sense of identification and appreciation for other peoples' viewpoints as well. When you discover that the way you see the world is utterly subjective, it begins to open possibilities and variety that didn't exist before. Empathy is the ability to realize this fact and understand the feelings and actions of other people.

The world shifts from right and wrong and black and white, to shades of gray all the time with many other points of view to consider. There may be things that might seem crazy or outlandish, or things that maybe you don't agree with, but you grow to accept a little bit more with information and education. This is fundamental to modern leadership. With great empathy comes great responsibility. Lack of empathy caused Past-Brett (and those around him) to have sleepless nights, blood-boiling fits of rage, and burned bridges.

That's the beauty about learning. It can only be done in two ways. You can either learn through experience and trial and error— sometimes that means catastrophic failure or financial disaster—or by guidance, mentorship, or coaching.

As a young leader, I learned the most from trial and error and by examining my experiences through introspection. When you're in your early twenties, you think you are invincible. Sometimes, the only way to disprove this theory is for the world to kick you really hard and tell you that you're wrong. All the advice from our parents, teachers, and coaches couldn't add up to altering the course we had already set for ourselves through that lens and experience.

Extraordinary results come when you combine tenacity with wisdom, and unfortunately, that is something few of us have when we do something for the first time.

The pain of failure is naturally the most realistic result. Of course, the more we learn through experience, and feel the pain that accompanies it, the more we realize that there is probably someone that has walked in our shoes and done this before. This is where the second way to learn comes in: Mentorship.

Find someone that has successfully done what you want to be doing and have them show you how. There is nothing new under the sun, so there's bound to be someone who can help you learn a better way of doing things. Often this is difference between the "working smarter" version of learning versus the "working harder" path. The relationship with a mentor will also grow your introspective skills and compound your results.

As a new founder, the earlier you can apply self-awareness on the pain that comes from early experiences, the faster you will move toward working smarter and seeking out guidance from others who have done what you want to be doing.

Establishing introspection in our lives is a powerful practice. It lays the foundation for all the hard and soft skill development that will need to take place to become the leader that will grow an organization. It is important to take the time and create an environment that is helpful for unpacking your thoughts and getting connected with your current lenses on the world.

Founder Tip

Find a quiet, distraction-free place to sit for two to four hours and spend that time dumping out all the thoughts, ideas, stresses, and tasks, that are on your mind. It's very helpful to create internal clarity and realignment, but also incredible for focusing on the next steps for moving forward. This should be done regardless if you are a solopreneur or have a team. I did this consistently once a month, with two sessions per year focusing on the big picture.

My recipe for success:

- quiet coffee shop
- no Wi-Fi—airplane mode on
- Drown out the noise with headphones instrumental music (I often looped one song to create consistency and focus).

Actively creating the headspace for introspection is a must for a new founder. The trap of being constantly reactive to what pops up every day in the business will never go away otherwise. Giving yourself this space to think will ensure you remain focused on the right things with your time and prioritize the most impactful tasks first.

Questions For The Business:

- What are the major parts of the business? (sales, marketing, production, customer service, etc.)

- What has been going well in each? Why?

- What is causing the most stress? Why? What is the source of that stress?

- What is the one problem that will make everything else easier if it gets solved? Why?

- What can happen today to make progress in solving that one problem?

Make sure to include the facts and data from the business, plus your emotions and feelings around the business. Both are important to your understanding and assessment.

Questions For You:

- What are my goals personally and professionally? (pick a specific timeline: year or month) Why?

- What will be the most challenging part about hitting those goals? Why?

- What will be the easiest part? Why?

- Does the current version of myself have the skills and capabilities to hit those goals? (If no, what are the gaps? Who or what can help fill them?)

- What is the one skill/habit/mindset change, that I can implement to make everything else easier?

- Would I follow me if I was employed by me? Why? Why not?

- If my title in the business disappeared, would my employees still follow me?

- What skills do I want to develop? Why?

- What areas of my life do I want to improve? Why?

- What does my ideal working day look like?

- What does my ideal day off look like?

Founder Summary

- Using the Why Filter
- Empathy and our unique lenses on the world
- Experience vs. Mentorship
- Give yourself the environment to be self-aware: use the template.

CHAPTER 2: THE SIX CORE HUMAN NEEDS

Now that we have the framework for looking inward and processing our thoughts, reactions, and decisions, let's discuss the building blocks for creating a common language that will help to contextualize and communicate this internal awareness.

Humans have an emotion-guiding system that is programmed within all of us and leads us to seek outcomes and make decisions in every moment of every day. Anthony Robbins popularized this idea and breaks down six core fundamental human needs that makes understanding why we do the things we do much easier.

When I was coaching my first high-performing entrepreneurs, I often didn't understand why I was drawn to certain types of people or repulsed by others. I didn't fully understand how someone could explain away not showing up to work on time consistently, or why others would, without fail, repeatedly give away their services for free or discount their prices.

What caused some to go out of their way to provide an exceptional client experience and work environment for their staff, while others always had difficulty getting paid and couldn't stop the revolving door of constant new employees? It all comes down to human needs and using our introspective skills to better interpret why we are drawn in certain ways and why the people around us make the decisions they do.

Robbins breaks down the six core human needs into four needs of the personality and two needs of the spirit. We are wired for all six, however there are usually two within the six that become a part of our main decision-making system and take the lead.

Personality Needs

Certainty

We all need some level of personal certainty as humans. If you don't know where your next meal is coming from, or if you're unsure if you'll have a roof over your head, it will be hard to think about much else. Having an acceptable degree of certainty in our lives makes it easier to think beyond compulsive survival toward what is possible. Once this threshold is met, then the need for certainty exists within a comfort zone.

Celine Certainty is a person who wants to know all the answers. She thrives when she has a pulse on every part of the project, because if she isn't the one doing it or overseeing it, something might go wrong and cause bigger problems. Celine wants to know the clearest path to get to where she wants; always searching for clarity and exploring "What Ifs." Black and white is less stressful than shades of gray. If it's not clear, or if the answers aren't immediately there, Celine won't take action until there is a clear way forward. She will begin with baby steps and move slow so she can see problems coming: mitigating risk.

Celine is hyper-organized. Clutter stresses her out and her daily tasks are mapped out to the highest degree. All this is for her peace of mind. Her friends sometimes poke fun at her because she is boring or a robot, but this certainty is the foundation for her to goals and sense of accomplishment.

Certainty is a core human need because it keeps us safe. Certainty provides the baseline to which many interpret as a comfort zone or having peace of mind. If certainty is pushed to its absolute limit, a life can feels boring or meaningless. Humans are problem-solving creatures, and if there isn't anything new to figure out, our lives may feel like there's a big hole; a missing piece to the puzzle. This is where optimizing everything particle of our lives and squeezing out opportunities for fulfillment becomes detrimental.

Variety

Variety exists at the opposite site of the certainty spectrum. We need variety to feel a sense of fulfillment through experiencing fresh ideas, seeing new perspectives, being introduced to different people, or travelling to other places.

Victor Variety is a "go with the flow" kind of guy. He will try anything once and is always yearning for adventure. He's constantly looking for something new. Victor loves discovering new music, a new local business, or a unique method for doing anything. Victor often leans into the future; for what's upcoming. "If it ain't broke, don't fix it," doesn't cut it for him. He loves sharing ideas, pushing the status quo, and he always has a vision. Since life is an adventure, his isn't well organized and planning isn't his thing.

Victor is the life of the party and has many friends that love when he is around. They probably think his ideas are crazy and doubt he will follow through. "Another one of his million-dollar ideas," they'll say—but he's got stories. Stories from where he has been, the people he has met, or the crazy thing he did.

Often, we live vicariously through the high variety people in our lives. "Wow I can't believe you did that," we may say or think. Most people love the more expected surprises, but people that have a high need for variety all have a love for the unexpected surprises as well: the unknown unknowns.

Without variety, our lives would be completely stale and lack meaning. However, taken to the extreme, too much variety feels like you're riding a high-speed runaway train you can't stop. This is why Certainty and Variety balance each other. Leading someone high in variety often means giving them the goal or defined result you're looking for and then allowing them to experiment and create the path to the goal for themselves. It might not be how you would have done it, and it might have taken slightly longer than you were hoping, but they will often come up with new ideas worth exploring for future projects. They will appreciate being given the leeway to experiment.

We need enough certainty in our lives to engage in new experiences, and we need enough variety and newness in our lives to engage in fulfilling problem-solving changes and a constant flow of the new.

Significance

We all need to feel important. The feeling of significance can be satisfied in several ways. On one side of the spectrum, significance can be fueled through validation of others. Buying fancy things, getting awards and compliments, pushing for promotions, and making more money are often external drivers for individuals with a high need for significance. Feeling significant can also come from praying, volunteering your time, or mentoring someone. The world acknowledges you, your presence, and what you can offer.

Sam Significance has always been a high achiever. In school, he played on numerous sports teams and was the captain of many of them. He pushed himself academically so he could have the top marks in the class and eventually became the valedictorian upon graduation. He went to law school because being a lawyer is what his family was hoping he would do. His salary at one of the top firms supported the lease of a brand-new Mercedes and the down payment on a luxury condo. It might have stretched him financially, but to him, it was important to look the part. He prided himself in having the answers and being the go-to guy. This would set himself up well for quickly climbing the ladder to become a partner.

His friends are mostly lawyers and professionals. Everyone likes Sam because he is smart, charismatic, and successful. He doesn't let a conversation go by without putting in his two cents and he likes to update everyone on what the latest and greatest addition to his life.

The need for significance is hardwired in all of us and humans crave acknowledgement and importance. We all want to feel like what we do is appreciated and valuable. Left unchecked, this driving force, however, can become unhealthy. Significance is interesting because it can be a massive, motivating fire that drives a lot of success in the eyes of others. But, if that success is only supported by the surface level opinions of others, it can become a recipe for a life with no sense of meaning or happiness.

Often the root of this need comes from a yearning to impress our parents or a family member from our childhood. That lack of validation or feeling of importance ultimately filters our adulthood decisions as we try and fill a love and connection void with superficial things. This is why love and connection are so important, and also why it's the fourth of our six core human needs.

Love/Connection

Our need for love and connection is one that a lot of us can make sense of intuitively. We are social creatures that thrive when we have meaningful relationships filled with love and appreciation. Connection balances the scales with our need for significance by directing where our energy goes. Our significance need draws energy toward us, while our need for connection and love gives energy away.

Carrie Connection is full of life. She is the first person to make sure everyone is included. She's is a fantastic listener and goes out of her way to help others in need. She sacrifices her own goals to help and serve others with theirs. She does everything in her power to avoid conflict and not damage the relationships involved. If conflict is unavoidable, she is the first responder to mitigate as much damage as possible and re-establish the harmony. Carrie puts a lot of value in the quality and deepness of her relationships and that holds true across her family, friends, and significant others.

Carrie's friends love her for how encouraging and helpful she is. They might say things like "she is always there when I need her," "she's so thoughtful," or "we've never fought."

When someone has a high-driving need for love and connection, they will often take on the weight of other's problems to make them feel better. Externally, everyone around them is elated and happy, but people like Carrie bottle up these emotions, conflicts, and burden and choose to process through it themselves so they don't damage relationships. This is where connection left unchecked can be detrimental. If Carrie continues to pour out all her energy serving the relationships around her and doesn't think about herself, this can lead to anger, resentment, and mental illness.

Finding a balance between significance and connection is so important. Significance allows us to focus on ourselves: our goals, our dreams, validation, and acknowledgement. Connection allows us to build lifelong relationships full of meaning where our goals and aspirations can thrive. As a founder, it's imperative to be actively thinking about this balancing act.

All four personality needs can show themselves in positive and negative ways. Each can serve us or hold us back, depending on how well we balance them. This is why having an awareness is so key.

Celine Certainty is meticulous and plans ahead, but can be overly controlling or miss out on opportunities.

Victor Variety is constantly uncovering new ideas and is up for exploring just about anything, but can be overwhelmed by a lack of planning, and his execution suffers.

Sam Significance has a hunger to get to the top, and that determination has served his achievements well. However, his definition of success is too strongly defined by people and factors that don't lead him to fulfillment.

Carrie Connection will go to the end of the earth for others and do everything she can to build deeper relationships. Taking on the problems of others at the cost of her own self-interest doesn't always support her sense of meaning.

Spirit Needs

Growth

We all have a need for growth. The feeling of making progress and development is a core driving factor in our happiness. Our need for growth is fueled and achieved through the four personality needs. Sam Significance feels growth when he is pursuing a meaningful goal that requires him to stretch and develop beyond his current skill set. Carrie Connection grows when she creates a deeper relationship.

The destination of growth is the feeling of fulfillment. This can mean mastery in a craft developed over years or decades. This can mean absolute clarity and certainty in who you are as an individual.

Growth is the path that our other needs walk down in search of happiness. A life that is standing still, free of problems to solve, with no finish lines to run toward, and people to do it with, will never be a truly fulfilled life. Growth is the reason why we seek out hard things and lean in when it gets tough. Growth is falling in love with the process to reach a goal so the achievement of that goal is sweeter. Growth can feel like being vulnerable despite your pride or ego. It can be saying "I love you" first. It can be skydiving to conquer your fear of heights. Growth is what underpins it all on a quest for meaning.

Contribution

Contribution serves our innate need to create lasting ripple effects with our lives. On the surface, contribution is often misinterpreted as a need to be selfless or serve. It's more ambiguous and harder to pinpoint. Although being selfless and helping others is part of it, I think contribution goes much deeper.

When you listen to what happy and fulfilled people have to say at the end of their lives, it always comes back to creating lasting impact and a legacy that extends beyond themselves as a single person. Their lives were not a zero-sum game, where the impact they had was only effective while they were here. Those that were the happiest and most fulfilled seemed to use their core needs to pursue goals that were greater than the sum of their parts. The accomplishments they had, the people they touched, and the value they created, extend far beyond checking off a bucket list. They inspired others toward action and impact.

Doing hard things has a lot more gravity when the driving "why" behind the goal has outcomes and by-products that extend beyond ourselves. Certainty, Variety, Significance, Connection, and Growth all work together to produce the relationships, goals, successes, organizations. These traits help create an impact that we can look back at the end of our lives and define as truly meaningful.

With a foundation of self-awareness and a greater understanding of what our core human needs are, we become better leaders. This foundation will make the decisions we make in our personal lives and the strategies we use within our businesses more focused. It gives us the tools to interpret our environment and relationships with more empathy. It also gives us more confidence as we grow to lean into our strengths and simultaneously develop our weaknesses.

Founder Summary

Six core human needs:

- Certainty
- Variety
- Significance
- Love/Connection
- Growth
- Contribution
- We all have them, but our strongest two impact the majority of our daily decisions and map the course for our lives.

CHAPTER 3: STRENGTHS, WEAKNESSES, AND THE SIXTEEN PERSONALITIES

Now that we have a foundation of self-awareness and an understanding of our six core human needs, the next step is to determine what our natural strengths and weaknesses are within this framework. This will help us gain a much clearer picture of how to lead ourselves and our eventual team.

I Imagine that if you're reading this book you're looking to improve and do things better. As a by-product of that, you're probably pretty hard on yourself since there are always things to improve on! I am definitely hard on myself. We all have strengths and weaknesses, but ultimately, we miss focusing on the strength part and lean more toward areas of improvement naturally. The first part of this chapter is about talking through strengths and creating a framework that will help dramatically with recognizing them in a deeper way. This is important because we often take them for granted or don't even know that we have them in the first place.

Growing up, I was hit semi-regularly with the phrase, "Are you good at everything?" I would usually smile and shrug it off with a slightly bigger head, but I didn't really know how to quantify it. As I moved from high school age into postsecondary education and then running my first business, I naturally took that mentality forward as a strength in most aspects since it gave me the feeling of confidence. I knew that I could just figure anything out. Of course, we all know how that turned out. It was blindly a blessing and a curse. It gave me uninformed optimism about my true skill set. The strength I had was larger in my head than in reality.

When I first started to get into leadership and business in a serious way, I was fortunate to be surrounded by a lot of amazing and talented people that were also starting on their entrepreneurship journey as well. I grew very quickly since I was able to absorb as much knowledge from my peers as possible in a short amount of time by actively participating in that environment, swapping stories, and seeking to understand how they solved more complex problems. It was mentorship on steroids and it skilled me up in a big way, fast.

On the flip side, without realizing it, while I was in a constant state of learning, I was also comparing myself to everyone around me. Not being the smartest guy in the room is a double-edged sword.

If I wasn't doing what they were doing, I was not successful.
If I didn't have the systems they did, I was not successful.
If I wasn't making as much money as them, I was not successful.

I filtered my decision making through what my peers would do. Because I was in a beginner phase of learning, truth be told, some of it really worked. Learning from my peers' mentorship and mistakes allowed me to not repeat them and I could see exciting growth. That's the beautiful thing about leveraging mentorship. However, there was a lot of things I tried to copy and implement that failed miserably. Looking back, it was all to do with our different strengths and weaknesses. I had a different style of leadership, management, and hiring, based on my internal wiring. Although some systems are universally helpful—like keeping track of expenses—how they run their businesses wasn't going to always work for me. As I progressed through the years, and my business grew, I realized that the way I needed to run my business needed to be in direct alignment with me so that I could double down on my strengths and delegate my weaknesses.

This chapter is going to focus on breaking down your strengths and your weaknesses so that you don't have to learn through experience and failure to learn how to be better as a leader and entrepreneur.

Strengths

Developing introspective skills and understanding your core needs, plus being able to gather feedback, will allow you to create a road map to your strengths and weaknesses much quicker. For myself, my main two driving needs are connection and significance. When building a company, this meant that I focused heavily on relationships and spent extra time getting to know my customers and employees. I made sure they were happy, that their goals were being met, and that they liked me more than the other entrepreneurs around me.

Being a good boss and a good leader was extremely important to me. I filtered a lot of my daily decision making through questions like "How can I improve the relationship?" or "Are they happy?" There's a natural harmony that is built into my mindset which proved to be very helpful for building culture and building trust when I was looking to scale my business beyond what I could solely control.

Your turn:

- What are your top two core needs?

- What areas of your life have you noticed these needs and recognized that they were really helpful?

- What do you get complimented on?

- Why do team members stay?

- What have your bosses raved about regarding your mind-set or performance?

- What results or situations filled you up with joy? Why?

Weaknesses

The by-product of having connection and significance as the main lenses I make decisions through can appear as me bending over backwards for other people—a lot like Carrie Connection. I want to strengthen the relationships and keep the harmony. This feels good for me, but it also means as an entrepreneur that I get paid, which reinforces my actions. That can be a negative catalyst for that good feeling.

I shot myself in the foot many times by making detrimental personal, financial, and growth decisions to keep the harmony of the team and the people around me. I did things like giving an employee a day off even if they didn't give proper notice or cracking under the pressure of an upset customer and giving them a discount. All of it came back to my need to feel important and significant without damaging the relationship.

Looking back, I probably could have saved a lot of stress, heartache, and money by having more awareness of my need for connection and significance. It was a hard lesson to learn, because within a thriving business, you'll never make everyone happy. Even when I managed to do so, it was always felt like the calm between storms. It's never sustainable because there are always problems in a business, especially if it's growing.

The best way to unpack and recognize your weaknesses is to do two main things:

First, have uncomfortable conversations with the positive people in your life. The thing about weaknesses is that we are our own worst critic by far. If we start asking ourselves "What am I bad at?" or "What do I need to improve on?" the answers aren't a true reflection of what the real areas of improvement are. This takes vulnerability and a bit of courage if you were like me and hadn't actively sought out feedback like this in the past. But, wow, it was worth it. One way to bring up the subject with your family, friends, colleagues, or boss is by prefacing the question with:

"I'm reading this book and developing my self-awareness skills. This might sound completely weird to hear, but I want your honest thoughts. What do you think I can improve on?"

It may be a bit scary, but most people respect the question. Vulnerability is a superpower and great leaders have it in spades.

Now, If you ask a difficult question; buckle in for difficult answers. These are most likely going to be people that you've known for years—maybe your whole life—and it is going to feel utterly strange getting negative feedback from them. If you are getting negative feedback from someone all the time, they're the wrong person to be asking this question.

I recommend having something to take notes on. It will give you a task to make it feel more objective, like research, and less like getting kicked in the gut. If you are not feeling a twinge of pain though, you aren't getting the unvarnished truth. This will be uncomfortable for them too, and they may try to soften the blow by sugarcoating their opinion. Just give them the permission to share openly.

After getting a minimum of two to four of these conversations completed, look back at your notes and start to find the patterns.

There are undoubtedly going to be some areas of overlap and that is what you want to focus on. The questions you ask yourself now will be much more impactful and focused around self improvement rather than fueling negative self-talk:

- How do my core needs show up in these themes?

- Are my self-defined weaknesses and the themes I collected different from the input of others?

- What are ways I can actively remind myself of these themes when they come up again?

- How will these themes show up in my business?

These conversations can lift the veil on a part of your world that you had no idea existed. It often strengthens relationships with those involved, and when you engage in it with the mentality of seeking to understand, not to judge, it can dramatically improve your daily decision making. However, if the very thought of asking this question to the closest people in your life scares you completely stiff with anxiety, a second option to consider doing first would be to take the Myers-Briggs personality test.

The Myers-Briggs Type Indicator is a self-assessment you can do online quickly to get a much deeper view on your strengths and weaknesses. It maps out sixteen separate personalities with unique indicators:

Analysts	Architect INTJ	Logician INTP	Commander ENTJ	Debater ENTP
Diplomats	Advocate INFJ	Mediator INFP	Protagonist ENFJ	Campaigner ENFP
Sentinels	Logistician ISTJ	Defender ISFJ	Executive ESTJ	Consul ESFJ
Explorers	Virtuoso ISTP	Adventurer ISFP	Entrepreneur ESTP	Entertainer ESFP

There are many ways to take the test, but one of the fastest is using 16personalities.com. It takes less than twenty minutes and, if you've never done tests like this before, will give you mountains of insight.

There are a lot of psychoanalytical online tests you can take, and many of them are absolutely incredible. For a fundamental starting point, this is the path of least resistance. It's my recommendation for anyone new to the introspection game because it's easy to understand and, in our case, builds off our Why Filters, personal lenses, and core needs extremely well. It gives us a common language to communicate this new knowledge with as well since a lot of business professionals use and understand it. For the record, I'm an ENFJ.

Founder Summary

- How have your top core needs helped you most in your life?
  Personally? Professionally?
- Take notes as you get meaningful, objective feedback from your closest positive relationships on areas to improve.
- Take the Myers-Briggs Type Indicator at www.16personalities.com

CHAPTER 4: MEANINGFUL GOALS TO RIDE THE CURVE

When you can start working toward a goal with the foundations we have discussed, it becomes a lot easier to make it meaningful and aligned to you. In today's world of constant exposure, and the hyperfiltered realities of social media, trying to set goals that satisfy your needs without the judgement of others creeping into our thoughts is challenging. With more awareness of our filters and core needs, plus useful knowledge of our strengths and weaknesses, it eases some of these negative comparisons and keeps us in our own lane.

Whether we are thinking about starting a business or have one already in motion, it is crucial that we define success. Let's put it in a box and draw a perimeter for ourselves, because "more clients," "more money," and "more recognition" is not a goal. That would be like starting a marathon without being told how far you have to run to complete it. It's impossible to train or prepare if all you're ever told is "just keep running."

When you know where you want to go, it's much easier to work smart and not just endlessly work hard. You can then begin with the end in mind and work backwards. You can create a path forward that best aligns with your strengths and your needs. You can eliminate layers of complexity by setting your markers for success early and being methodical. This allows for momentum to gather as you build up small wins because you know how to define a small win. These small wins will serve the big wins, and therefore you get closer to your definition of success. It's so much more actionable!

When things go wrong, or unforeseen problems come up, you can measure them against something and determine if it's a small problem or a big problem. If you are blindly moving forward with no compass or reference point, every problem is going to feel like a massive problem, when, in reality, most really aren't. A clear definition of success gives you the litmus test to measure all your decisions up to and remain objective.

> *"You can't manage what you don't measure."*
> *– Peter Drucker*

Goals can be any length and to create goals that have meaning and alignment, start big and then figure out the shorter-term goals afterward. Navigating a dense forest is easier when you can look out in all directions from the tallest tree first. My suggestion is to begin with yearly goals, then quarterly goals, then monthly, then weekly, etc. What you spend your time on every day has direct alignment to hitting the weekly goal, which will serve in hitting the monthly goal, which will hit the quarter, and the quarters will hit the goal for the year. This method makes each day much more actionable. The only way to eat an elephant is one bite at a time.

Example:

Meaningful yearly goal: $100,000 in revenue

Quarterly goal: $25,000 in revenue

Monthly goal: $8,334 in revenue

Weekly goal: $1,924 in revenue

A weekly goal of $1,924 is much more achievable than the more daunting figure of $100,000 per year.

If you have a house-painting business like I did, all you need to do that week is find one house to paint for $1924 or more. If you consult for $100/hour, all you need to do is have 19.24 billable hours. By breaking down our goals into the simplest terms, they become easier to navigate and achieve. This keeps us focused on the work and the process versus living in a world of blind faith hoping that the massive contract we proposed comes through. Plus, if that big job doesn't come through, it won't take the wind out of your sails and slow down your momentum. Since you've been consistently chalking up small wins, you are still working toward your bigger goals every day.

If you need help framing the right questions to set meaningful goals for a new business, here are some suggestions:

- What are the projects you would regret not pursuing/achieving? What are the ideas that keep you up at night?

- What would going through the process in pursuit of that project teach/give you?

- What is your definition of success for the goal?

- What's in it for Future-You if you get it done?

- How much money do you need monthly to cover all your costs, including having fun?

- What would you do with your days if all of those costs were paid already?

- What activity do you get lost in for hours?

Ask yourself these questions if your business already has some momentum:

- What are the revenue and profit numbers your business would need to hit to make you grin ear-to-ear and lose sleep? Why those numbers specifically?

- What does your ideal workday look like when you're hitting those metrics?

- Can you accomplish these results with your current team?

This will help to put a clear finish line on your definition of success. Without it, you will just be running that endless marathon. When we think about what is truly valuable to achieve in our lives, personally and professionally, and we can define how it will look and feel to arrive there, making a clear plan back to now becomes much easier and exciting.

Now, this isn't to say it won't be challenging; it absolutely will be from time to time. As an entrepreneur, growing pains happen through constant problem solving. Any time we embark on anything new in our lives, we go through a natural series of emotions that cycle over and over. As we learn, adapt, and undercover new opportunities or problems, it repeats. This cycle is called the Transition Curve and it's a fundamental building block within the foundation of true self-awareness. Based on Don Kelley and Daryl Conner's Emotional Cycle of Change model from the mid-1970's, the Transition Curve is made up of six key points.

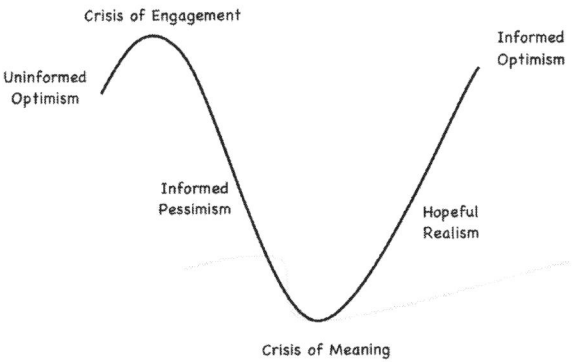

Uninformed Optimism: We start something completely new or start a new part of a process we don't know what we don't know and have blind excitement. We may think a task will take an hour to complete, but someone more experienced knows it will take five hours. Dramatically underestimating the difficulty of a new process is an easy example of uninformed optimism.

Crisis of Engagement: This is the "Oh, Crap!" moment. It's that sinking feeling when the fog clears, and you realize the actual size of the mountain you are climbing. You are in over your head and have so much more work in front of you than you expected.

Informed Pessimism: The quick descent of emotion after the shock of the crisis of engagement or the down in the dumps feeling when you question why you decided to start in the first place. This is often where a lot of negative self-talk pops up as you process through it. It might be frustration, tears, hopelessness, or something else for you, but this is a dark place of doubt and uncertainty.

Crisis of Meaning: This is the moment of decision. Fight or flight. This is where you decide to either get back up and dust yourself off or throw in the towel.

Hopeful Realism: This is the state after you decide to fight. There's energy behind you again to charge forward with the goal you have put in front of yourself. However, this time you have a newly found confidence that didn't exist before. You know what you're up against, and you're okay with it. You're ready to get it done.

Informed Optimism: This is the buildup of realistic excitement before another problem pops up. The cycle now begins again.

These transition curves will be numerous and ongoing throughout the entrepreneurship journey, as well as in all parts of our lives. We might be at Hopeful Realism within our business, but our family situation might be in a Crisis of Meaning. Even within our business, we might be feeling Hopeful Realism at the big picture level, but maybe at the Informed Pessimism stage at the small scale after a client sent you an angry email the day before.

Transition curves are a fact of life and the more we can use our introspective skills and knowledge to realize where we are within them, the easier and faster it will be to push through. This self-awareness also reduces the magnitude of the emotions we experience while moving through the wave of a transition curve. The goal is tiny ripples, not an angry ocean. This is a muscle that will strengthen over time the more it is used.

Building a business is a slow burn that takes a lot of tenacity, passion, and a big focus on growth. The more meaningful and aligned your short-term and long-term goals are, the more you'll enjoy the process itself. If you enjoy the process and implement the self-awareness foundations we have discussed, your transition curves will be much more manageable when problems inevitably arise. The finish line is always at the top of Informed Optimism, so stick with it.

Now it's time to build a team.

Founder Summary

- Clearly define success and create a finish line to know exactly
  when you get there.
- Meaningful goals should start big and finish small to make them aligned and actionable.
- Use the Transition Curve to internally map out where you are. Use it often and problems disappear more quickly.

SECTION 2:
TEAM BUILDING & ASSEMBLY

CHAPTER 5: PREFERENCES & ABILITIES

Building a team is a whole lot easier once you know what direction you are headed. The foundations we've discussed up to this point have given you the tools to understand yourself and build an aligned vision. To achieve the vision, assembling a team is critical—but that focus needs to extend into your selection process. This chapter is going to focus on choosing talent that serves that alignment, not how to interview specifically. There are countless books for that. We want to have specific conclusions we are looking for, so that the questions being asked have a direction and purpose.

Every person has eight criteria that you can look for while picking your team. They can be further divided up into three innate abilities and five personal preferences.

Ability	Values	Fundamental	Instrumental

Preference	Attainment	Tenacity	Leadership
	Precision	Introspection	

Abilities

Values:

This element is relatively self-explanatory. Will they make morally correct decisions? How do they treat others around them? How do those people react to their decisions? Do I trust them? Will they fly your flag with pride? Will they do what they say they will do?

Values are something that should be a line in the sand. It should absolutely be a deal breaker. If the person you're sitting across from doesn't agree with your definition of doing the right thing, they won't be a good fit. Don't try and change them. You simply don't have time. People might change over long periods of time, but it will be far less painful for you and them to find someone else that aligns with you and train them instead. Skills are easier to teach than values.

I've had some of my worst experiences with employees that had a lot of technical skills and experience, but also had bad values. I had some of my best experiences with employees that were in sync with my values, but had little to no skill or experience. I was happy to train and build their skill levels.

Employees with misaligned values will be the never-ending thorn in your side. They will be the toothache that doesn't go away. It's not worth it.

Fundamental Ability:

This is someone's ability to keep on going and persevering. It's the ability to weather the storm in the face of adversity and how much pain you can endure in the pursuit of a goal. Will the candidate endure short-term pain for longer-term gains? How do they manage their mood when problems pop up? Fundamental ability is the baseline of internal wiring.

If someone has a strong fundamental ability, they will be able to learn more, adapt quicker, and be more receptive to change and feedback. There are very few cases where having a low fundamental ability is advantageous, however, depending on the nature of the role you are hiring for, a lower level of fundamental ability isn't always a deal breaker.

Instrumental Ability:

Instrumental abilities are the basic life skills like manners, reading ability, and common sense. This person has a firm handshake, can make eye contact, and has a degree of social emotional intelligence. First impressions fall into this ability category. The way someone is dressed, the way they smile, and the way they interact with others around them is all instrumental ability. Would they represent you and your business they way you want? Would you be embarrassed at all?

Depending on the role you're hiring for, the acceptable threshold for instrumental ability is different. I've moved cross-country multiple times and the best moving experience of my life was with a company that often hires people who can't read. I had a math professor who had multiple PhDs, yet couldn't hold a simple conversation for more than a few seconds, making it incredibly difficult to ask questions and learn. The acceptable level of instrumental ability you determine will be based on the role you are filling.

Preferences

Attainment:

This is the internal wiring to pursue and achieve goals. A candidate that has a high preference for attainment will often have important milestones that they're working toward all the time. They will consistently have a plan on how to hit those goals; whether it be personal or professional.

High attainment means the candidate is willing to put in the hours to succeed with the goals they put in front of themselves. They practice and have a find-a-way mentality when they hit a roadblock.

Depending on the role you're hiring for, the minimum level of attainment that fits the role will be different, but employees with average or above average attainment make it much easier to align your goals with them. They will take ownership of the task at hand and make a plan to hit the outcomes you need by appropriate deadlines. They already have this drive because it is part of their internal wiring.

This isn't to say that it will be easy to get their buy-in all the time. It may sometimes be difficult because they haven't yet found a meaningful way to connect your goals to theirs. Often, if you are vulnerable and share your insight and talk it through, they will lean in and reciprocate. Alignment is key. Without it, the potential you can get out of high attainment employees won't be fully realized.

Tenacity:

These candidates can grind. They don't stop until the job is done and all loops are closed. They don't quit when it gets tough. This is an individual that can push through, work hard, and put in serious sweat equity. Depending on the role you're hiring for, high tenacity is going to be defined differently. A construction worker lifting heavy materials six days a week shows a different kind of tenacity than a computer programmer working all night long to hit a release deadline. Before you begin hiring employees, define what true hard work is going to look like in an ideal world so you have a benchmark to measure against.

Leadership:

Having a high preference for leadership means that you can comfortably take charge, organize next steps when direction is needed, help process group decision making, and actively reach out to support others that need `one-on-one guidance.

Candidates with a high preference toward leadership are comfortable making difficult decisions. This means occasionally going against the grain and deciding to go left when the group wants to go right. They can separate the objective need from the emotional opinions to make the best decision.

Leadership may or may not be required for every role. Some of my best employees were terrified of taking the lead and just wanted to take full ownership of the task I gave them. All of your employees don't have to demonstrate high leadership skills. If they did, you will have too many chefs in the kitchen. But, as your business grows and you expand past your capacity to juggle everything, a select few employees with a high preference for leadership become invaluable.

Precision:

This is a high preference toward organization and orderliness. Precision means a high capacity for systems thinking, seeing how components are connected, and the ability to execute efficiently. Candidates with high precision usually have color-coded calendars and flawless morning routines. They know exactly where they need to be, when they need to be there, and what they will need once they arrive.

Employees with precision won't be late and will want to have a plan before being fully bought into your goals and vision. Once that clarity is achieved, they will be loyal and faithful. You may find they struggle in work environments that are subject to constant unexpected changes. People with precision like to have consistency and room to plan ahead for changes. Depending on the role you are filling, having employees that prefer precision may or may not be a large factor that influences employee success.

Introspection:

The last preference is one that we've already spent a lot of time talking about. A candidate that has strong introspective preferences will be able to tell you what their strengths and weaknesses are. Often these candidates have gone through life experiences that have helped develop their self-awareness. These people are probably familiar with tools like Myers-Briggs and the six core needs. They can give examples in their life that shape who they are and how that impacts their performance.

Often is a job interview, candidates are scared to answer the questions that focus on weaknesses. If your candidate has a high preference for introspection, they most likely won't have a problem with a deeper discussion. This is almost universally a preference that when higher, results are better.

I've put together a one page PDF chart for interviewing to make this process easy and streamlined. Go to bretthilker.com/interviewchart to download it.

When you are sitting down with each candidate, give them a score of one to ten on each of the abilities and preferences. Then after the interview, compare your notes and scores to the ideal version you've created. You can keep these scores to yourself and don't need to show the candidate. You're running a business, not judging Olympic diving!

Make sure to set boundaries on what your deal breakers are. If a candidate does not meet basic requirements, don't spend anymore time with them. Politely inform them that they are not a good fit. Then they can quickly move on to find a role that will be better for them and you can quickly move on to another candidate. No hurt feelings.

Don't get caught up in the story a candidate has about why they're different and why you should make a compromise. Make a deal with yourself before starting interviews that you will not compromise on these deal breakers. You have spent the time carefully deciding exactly what you need in an employee. Trust yourself and your insight. Anyone that falls short won't be the person you would want to fly your flag or go to war for you. Learn through my pain—it's not worth it!

Founder Summary

- Eight preferences and abilities for hiring
- Start with values: If you get that right, everything is easier.
- Spend time creating the ideal employee to use as a reference point to compare your candidates to during the interview process.
- Create deal breakers and don't compromise.

CHAPTER 6: THEMES IN THE TEAM

Your team is now blossoming after you were diligent with sifting through the preferences and abilities of the candidates. When you decide on specific attributes to look for and set your deal breakers, you give yourself the best chance finding your ideal employees. The by-product of using these preferences and abilities as filters is that you eliminate a lot of the guesswork that goes into standard interviews.

However, the other by-product is that there may be some themes that you notice within your employees' needs. If you have implemented the Myers-Briggs personality test in your process, you will still need to ensure the puzzle pieces that you've picked actually fit together in a productive way to hit your goals. Just because you have the strongest bricks doesn't mean you can stack them any way you like and build something tall and strong. We need to be methodical.

When you bring on anyone new, have them do a core needs assessment and a Myers-Briggs test. If they have never done a test like this, it may be weird for them, and you will probably have to give them more direction about completing the test. Sometimes people view self-awareness tests like these as actual tests with right and wrong answers and not an exercise in self-discovery. You will need to be more committed to it than they will be at first in order to get it done. But trust me, this bit of extra effort will be worth it. They'll thank you.

This will arm them with knowledge that has been untapped up to this point in their lives. This kind of insight can be applied everywhere, often having positive effects not just professionally, but personally.

Without the clarity and understanding that comes from this work, it makes it more difficult for you to create an environment in which they can thrive from day one.

On the flip side, if a new employee has already done these self-examinations, you will want to navigate next steps in a different way. If they've done it recently, take time to sit down and talk it through. This is most likely one of your hires that scored high in Introspection and would most likely enjoy having a discussion about it in a deeper way beyond an interview setting.

Before giving your thoughts on anything, make sure to start by asking for their thoughts first. This will leave the conversation open ended and let them freely discuss how they interpret their own self-awareness without judgement of how you frame it. This is going to be a good litmus test to see if you are both on the same page about their role on the team.

Make sure to be open in sharing your journey and personality discoveries with them as well. This will build trust and create a bond between the both of you that can be very beneficial once day-to-day work begins. Now, discussing where you see them fitting in is much easier and they are much more open to your feedback.

If they haven't done the tests in a while, I would have them do it again as a refresher. If it's been a while, there may be some subtle differences between who they are now versus when they originally took it. This will give you the clearest results and it will be affirming for them to see that nothing has changed or, if something has, it will be validating for them that they retook it. This rediscovered alignment will be a big leverage point in building your relationship with them once work begins.

When you have all of theses conversations with each of your employees and you've collected the data, spend time looking at all of it side-by-side. Undoubtedly, there will be themes that pop out.

Maybe you hired mostly extroverts or half of your people have a high need for variety while the other half have a high need for growth. There is no perfect answer on how this mix should look. What is more important is that you know and use that knowledge to make better decisions moving in working with the team.

From my experience, most entrepreneurs hire people that are like them to some degree. This is common and totally natural, because all of us want to spend our time around people we genuinely enjoy being around. Since you're going to be spending a lot of time with your employees, you'll definitely want this familiarity in some capacity. Just be aware that you may have a tendency to spend more time around people you relate to more, and make sure you don't neglect the others. They still need your support, guidance, and leadership. They are talented and a great fit for the job based on what you're looking for; they just have different needs and personality indicators.

I'm an ENFJ with high core needs for connection and significance, so I tended to hire extroverted people who leaned to the connection side of needs. This wasn't everyone, but it was always higher than average. I tended to gravitate toward these employees naturally, and I needed to check myself from time to time and ensure I was also looking after the needs of my other employees that were more introverted or had higher needs for certainty or variety.

Your people are your building blocks. Based on the preferences and abilities you've decided are important, these building blocks are still a similar shape. They have a different composition of materials formed into that shape and it's important to be aware of the make-up of each of your people. Don't assume that just because everyone you hired scored a seven or above in tenacity that they're going to all work hard together in the same way and be on the same wavelength while doing that hard work.

When you understand what factors have formed your team members into who they are, it is much easier to lead them individually. With an understanding of everyone's personality, preferences, and needs, connecting the right employees together and using one person's strength to support other's weaknesses becomes easier to implement. As a result, you'll see more growth, more quickly.

Have an orientation day with everyone you hired and see who gravitates toward each other. This is an easy way to get everyone together and onboard everyone with the company vision, but also to see how their needs and personalities fit within the group.

Discuss the exercise and discover their needs and personality types. This creates an open space for your new employees to get to know one another and also lets the group know how they filter the world individually. This greater understanding for each other will immediately strengthen the working relationships among them and also create an environment where sharing these ideas is accepted. Moving forward, it creates a common language where they can address situations or conflict by easily communicating how they are processing through it from that place of understanding and self-awareness.

> "I'm sorry, I'm just being a high J right now."
>
> "The extrovert part of me wants to do that."
>
> "My high certainty just really wants to know what the plan is."

Establishing the common language of core needs and personality types as a foundation means that problems are solved faster, with less tension, and greater empathy. This keeps business momentum moving, strengthens relationships, and reduces turnover by eliminating a lot of the surface level disconnects and frustration that happen in the workplace.

The number one reason people leave jobs is a sour relationship between their manager and their coworkers. This deeper understanding of each other greatly reduces the chances of your employees leaving for surface level issues. This also means that when new employees are added to the team later, it will be easier to integrate them with this common language as a foundation. Culture becomes stronger and new employees are accepted into the culture faster.

Put employees together that can feed off of each other's strengths and naturally gravitate toward each other. An easy example is that extroverts generally work well together, since they can process the work they're doing externally and bounce ideas off one another, while introverts also work well together, since they are comfortable processing among themselves. This doesn't mean that combining these different types of people won't work—because it absolutely can—but it's a good starting point.

The next thing to consider is combining people with planning and execution traits. You will need a degree of leadership within all of your sub-teams, as well as a balance of certainty and variety to balance innovation and planning. This can be said for balancing high Ps and high Js as well.

When thinking of specific projects that you will take on, these combinations will be especially important to consider. If you have a client that needs something done exactly the way she sees it or else, you won't want high variety, high-perceiving members of the team on that contract. They will get bored, overwhelmed, and behind on the deliverables, and start to resent the client. If a customer is all about the interactive experience and he enjoys the collaboration with the team, high extroverts and high connection will be a great fit.

If employees love to work with each other, but the project needs direction and they have lower leadership, bringing in someone else on the team higher in significance and stronger in leadership to work with them and get everything moving forward. The new teammate on the project is recognized for stepping in, and the realignment with the work makes everyone happy, including the client.

There is always going to be a degree of trial and error with these collaborations and you'll need to be open to shuffling things around to find the right combinations. Keep communicating with your team and talking things through as you make changes.

Everyone can work together to move the business forward as a cohesive unit.

Founder Summary

- Have everyone go through discovering their core needs and personality type.
- A more introspective team creates a common language and an environment of more open communication.
- There will be some personality themes. Group your sub-teams according to how they feed off of each other and balance leadership, planning skills, and idea generation effectively depending on project and/or client.

CHAPTER 7: THE RIGHT PEOPLE DOING THE RIGHT THINGS

After some trial and error, there will be some people on your team that naturally are good or improve at specific tasks. Within the day-to-day ecosystem of your business, pay attention to who likes doing what and who continually drops the ball on, or avoids, certain tasks. This is going to give you much more certainty in putting the right team members on the right tasks to get the job done effectively the first time around without as much hand-holding from you (we'll discuss proper delegation a little later).

Since your team knows that you are going to be trying different combinations to start out, it won't come as a surprise if you make changes on roles or tasks. If you frame it as a good thing—an opportunity to try out as many tasks in the business as possible—no one will see it as a failure or insult to be moved to a different area.

Running a painting company, I gave my different crews the opportunity to work on different kinds of projects. Every week for the first month, I also used the data I collected by interacting with my new staff out in the field the previous week to purposefully shuffle my crew members around and have different people work with each other to find the combination that would produce the best results. This also resulted in the happiest customers and the most excitement from my staff. Use your intuition for this as you've already interviewed, on-boarded, and oriented everyone together. There will be some combinations that just make sense.

Within those crews, I would often let each crew member lead the job site for a half-day period to see how their leadership preferences blossomed within the context of my business. Sometimes, I was pleasantly surprised. Other times, I was let down from what I saw. But, that's the importance of doing this. The quicker you can rinse these things out, the faster you can discover a better fit and adjust people, roles, and expectations to where everyone is firing on all cylinders and loves doing it.

In my world, there were people on the team that really enjoyed planning projects and picking up supplies. Others despised it and just wanted to get things done. Some employees loved talking with customers and making sure they were happy. Others found every excuse in the book to not talk to customers. When you spend the initial days and weeks with your people on the front lines seeing how they react to workday situations, you gain a lot more confidence to shuffle things around with the assurance that when you're not there, your team can avoid unexpected pitfalls If you're entrepreneurial like me and have always done everything yourself, this is going to give you the peace of mind to trust the people you've brought on.

Make sure to get their feedback too. Since you've established open communication among your team from the beginning, asking what people are liking and loving will be easier. I would start one-on-one with each new employee at the beginning of the following week. This allows the short-term emotion and biases of the previous week to not affect the feedback you get. You will get more objective answers on Monday morning versus Friday afternoon.

In the first month of working any new job, the more interaction you can have between your people and you, the better. It will show them you care and simultaneously allow them to iron out their own expectations and working relationship with you in a comfortable environment. When they know you'll be checking in with them, they can have the peace of mind. They know that if there's something they need to say, the pressure is off their shoulders to hunt you down or wait for the perfect moment to lay it on you. This way they can focus on their work without the feedback festering, and you don't get unexpectedly hit by a freight train of things to improve on or do differently. This actively planned time to hear feedback also keeps your transition curves a more manageable size.

There will be a lot of conversations that go really well. Employees may tell you what has gone well, how much they loved working with a specific person, or what they learned that week that makes them excited. There will also be conversations that are a mixed bag of good and bad, plus a small number that will be pretty negative. This is going to happen.

It's better that the negative feedback is being communicated in a way that both of you can have a conversation about it. If it is mostly negative feedback, it means that the team member has spent a lot of time throughout the week collecting their own examples and data points. By the time it comes to you, it's going to feel like they're opening the floodgates. Just listen. Seek to understand, not to reply. They have been waiting all week to discuss these things, so give them the time to get it all out. In these conversations, spend 80 percent of your time listening and 20 percent speaking. They just want to be heard. Once they've got everything out and explained the issues, only then is it appropriate to share your thoughts without breaking trust or coming across as defensive.

"I appreciate your vulnerability sharing that with me, I know it can be tough. Can I share my thoughts?"

That's powerful. It acknowledges them, shows you were listening, respects their point of view, and creates a two-way street where you can share your thoughts by framing it as a question.

After this conversation happens, it is incredibly important that you both have very clear next steps to implement afterward. If the conversation is just a feelings exchange or venting session it's going to be a broken record experience all over again in a week. Get very clear about what they can do, and what you can do to improve for this week (remember, it's Monday) and have additional talks with them before next week.

If they don't like who they were working with, understand why and make the necessary changes. If they don't like the level of responsibility they were given, give it to someone else. The whole point of intentional and frequent check-ins like this is to have these pain points feel like a stubbed toe instead of a toothache. They both hurt, but pain from a stubbed toe lasts for a few minutes, while a toothache can be days, weeks, or months. If you add up all the pain, the toothache sucks a lot worse.

As the entrepreneur, actively lean into these changes, until your weekly touch points become mostly positive (it will never be 100 percent), and the negative feedback is easy and surface level fixes. If specific team members still complain, and changes have been made, it will be a sign that he or she is not a good fit for your business.

You can do the very best job interviewing, looking for preferences and abilities, creating a common language with needs and personality types, checking in weekly, making changes, and creating a fit, but sometimes, it simply just isn't working. We're all human and there will always be this margin of error. This is the challenge and the beauty of building your empire. Your goals will never happen in a straight line. If you work hard and prepare, there will be minor speed bumps rather than major walls.

Founder Summary

- Expose new employees to all angles of your business and have them interact with other team members.
- The faster you can get a sense of what they lean toward, the faster you can get maximum effectiveness and happiness in a role that best helps the team and the business.
- Weekly check-ins to gauge what they like and don't like for the first month will give you the insight to make strategic changes for the better. Rinse and repeat to iron out the kinks.
- Some people you thought would be a good fit, won't be. And that's okay.

CHAPTER 8: THE NEW WORK-LIFE BALANCE

In this age of ever-growing connectedness, the line between life and work is becoming more and more fuzzy. Gone are the times when most of us can "clock out" at the end of the day or on Friday afternoon before the weekend and not have work left over that could be done. Sometimes, it's even expected that we take work home with us, literally or figuratively.

This is something you'll need to consider with your team. You didn't just hire their talents, and strengths, but you've also hired their personal obligations. It's easy to say, "keep your personal life at home when you're working," but:

- Most people don't have the mental strength to keep these separate.
- You will break the trust in the relationship that you've established if you draw that hard line in the sand—it's not realistic or sustainable.

After you've gone through all this effort to hire, train, and shape your team, up to this point, it is critical that you can establish a connection between each of your employee's work goals and their personal goals. This might sound counterintuitive at first, but it needs to happen if you want to build employees up for the long term.

This process can be started right after you hire someone or some time in the onboarding process after a few weeks on the job. Depending on the nature of your business, it will fluctuate. My business was very seasonal, so I found it advantageous to have these conversations sooner versus later, since time was a precious resource. But for others, building something that has constant momentum without being at the will of nature, this could happen a few weeks in without missing much.

Most employees are comfortable sitting down and discussing goals and alignment with you since you've created an atmosphere of open communication. Regardless of when it happens, having an open environment where they can be free to express things like personal goals is a must. If they're not comfortable sharing, it's a sign the trust between you and them has not become strong enough to warrant the conversation. I found this to be rare, but it did happen. Make sure to clearly communicate why it's important for you to understand what they are working toward personally and professionally so that you can do the best you can to support them in both while they are a part of your team.

When they are ready, the conversation is relatively straightforward. Spend time discussing what they are working toward long term personally and why that is important to them. Break the long term into a one-year (or one-season in my case) goal that would serve the bigger picture at the end of the year. Like we did in Chapter 4, work backwards with them to creating quarterly, monthly, and weekly goals showing them how it all will connect. Sometimes, this is the first time a person has ever been this intentional thinking about their "dreams," but your job is to give them a plan and make it bite-size and actionable. This will get them on top of the transition curve if they can see how the small steps will serve the medium ones, and the medium ones will serve the longer-term ones.

Next, you want to connect these new personal goals they have to your business and how it can help. Often, there are skills that you can teach them and work with them to develop that will help achieve the goals they have. Learning planning and scheduling, leadership, handling conflict, or processing through stress are all skills I've connected to the goals of past employees through their work experience with me and how I coached them.

Sometimes it can be as simple as an employee having a certain amount of money they want to make. What they get paid working for you will go directly toward paying for the thing they're saving up for. I've had multiple employees over the years (one of them being my younger sister) working to save up for travelling abroad. We figured out what the whole trip would cost including flights, accommodations, spending cash, etc., and then reverse engineered how many hours and how many projects she would need to complete that season working for me. We looked at her taking on extra work on the weekend and after working on her leadership skills, to be promoted to site-manager with a pay raise. At the end of the season, she had more than she needed to go on her trip and not worry about money.

When you can connect someone's personal long-term goals to short-term actions at work, they have a deeper sense of connection between their work life and their professional life. When they do hit the medium- and long-term goals, all the short-term work (and the inevitable headaches that come along with it) will be easier to manage because in their mind it all serves a purpose.

They are happy because you cared enough to help them connect the dots, and you're happy because the work they're completing for you has more meaning than it just being a transaction of putting time in to get money out. I've had employees reach out to me years after moving on from my business and express nothing but gratitude for the time they spent with me.

When our daily actions can build toward bigger things for our future, our memory has this funny trick of dissolving the pain away and only leaving the growth and relationships behind. This is why a holistic business environment that aligns the professional and the personal for the long term is greater than the sum of its parts. This also creates a more fruitful environment to build a tight-knit and sustainable performance culture among your team.

Founder Summary

- Spend the time connecting each employee's personal goals
  with their professional goals working for you.
- This creates greater meaning behind the work they do with you and the alignment makes transition curves easier to process through for your people.

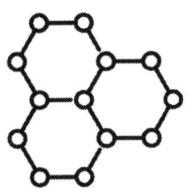

SECTION 3:
THE BUILDING BLOCKS
OF CULTURE

CHAPTER 9: EMPATHY & VULNERABILITY

The fire's burning now. There are incredible people on the team, they're in the right roles, and they understand how they are wired. There's alignment between your goals and theirs, and the right work is getting completed; A feeling of momentum. The wheels are turning. The next step is to accelerate forward. That isn't polishing up the business plan, working more hours, or jumping into another round of hiring. In fact, it's not strategy focused at all. The next step is taking the foundations that have been established with your people and building a performance culture among them. This is adding massive fuel to the fire.

"Culture eats strategy for breakfast." – Peter Drucker

In today's world of leadership and building businesses, the only way to achieve sustainability with your team and to achieve a whole that is greater than the sum of its parts is to lead through empathy and vulnerability. Long gone are the days of the crack-the-whip styles of leadership from the 1970s and 1980s where people would listen and oblige their superiors out of respect for the title. Not anymore.

The only way that you can create and environment where people stay long term, and continually do incredible work, is very clearly communicate with them that you're imperfect—that you're not superhuman. In the twenty-first century, that is how you create bonds where your team full-out goes to war for you.

This might sound funny and counterintuitive, but there's so many people that try and lead teams by projecting a facade of perfection. Since no one is perfect, it might feel good in the moment to command that respect, but, it's a losing battle. It's inevitable that you won't have an answer, make a mistake, miscount, forget, or have bad judgement at some point. All the work you've put into maintaining a scratch-free exterior will crumble in a moment, along with the respect from those that look up to you in that form. So why put yourself through having to rebuild that trust? Start with authenticity and everything is easier.

When I first started as a young founder, I had taken cues from the people around me, as we all do when we try something new. I copied my initial leadership style for my business from past sports coaches, my parents, teachers I respected, and characters in movies. The problem was the source of where *they* were drawing their leadership inspiration: from those days gone by, when the name plate of the desk mattered more than the relationship. So, when I absorbed what I saw and transplanted those old ideas into a new business, it very quickly led to unhappy people, lack of trust, and a revolving door of turnover. I wanted to have the final say and I wanted the control. I wanted my employees to respect me because I hired them and I trained them. After all, my name was on the contracts.

Wow, I wouldn't have worked for that guy. See ya!

When you become the go-to person, the hub at the center of the wheel where every decision hinges on you, you indirectly train your team how stuff gets done. It eliminates the ownership of decision making from anyone else and can take the wind from your team's sails. This won't happen overnight, but for them it will eventually feel like stunted growth; that where they've been planted (your business) won't allow them to flourish and reach their potential. This approach does not inspire confidence for modern employees that want to do meaningful work that can fulfill their needs for growth and contribution.

As the white knight with all the answers, you also put a speed limit on how fast your business can grow. You only have twenty-four hours in a day, and, within that, there are only so many decisions that can be made. Some of them will be really important, and some decisions won't be. But, if the expectation is that you are the decision gatekeeper, the business will eventually get to a point where the amount of decisions that need to be made will outweigh the amount you can physically make in any given time period.

For me, this meant stepping way outside my comfort zone and dismantling my shields. The pain of constantly feeling like an actor in my own play and the pain of endlessly hiring and retraining new employees now outmatched the pain of me letting my guard down and allowing my employees in. Scaling was more important than my ego.

What's funny is that it was my first business. Everyone knew it was. So why was I trying so hard to convince everyone around me that I had it all figured out when there was no expectation that I should have?

Today, respect comes from being vulnerable and open to the challenges that you have. People respect the willingness to work through challenges more than not having them in the first place. Everyone has challenges, and the simple acknowledgement of the ones you have builds instant trust. On top of that, when your team sees an imperfect person willing to push past those challenges, lead them, do hard things, and pursue a vision, they respect you even more.

No one expects perfection. What they expect from a leader is to learn, adapt, and grow without straying from what's important: your integrity and your goals. "Fake it to you make it" is dead. When the little rectangle in our pocket holds any answer to any question we can think of, leadership today doesn't mean the one who has the most knowledge. Our BS-filters are too strong now.

Leadership today means being the person that shows others how to accomplish what they thought wasn't possible. It's chasing down a vision and bringing others along for the ride because it moves them, too. It's about connection. It's about creating an environment where everyone is growing through meaningful work and our pocket-rectangles are just useful tools to help us accomplish it.

Your team doesn't need you for your knowledge; your team needs you for your guts. They need you to make the hard decisions. They watch you weather the storm with a grin and a plan when everything is on fire. They don't need you to be a human Google. They need you to be there for support and understanding when they make a mistake. They want someone to follow that will respect them, train them, give them certainty when it's missing, and hope for the future where they have a role within it. It's not about perfection.

To get this done, start by admitting when you've screwed up. When you make a mistake, acknowledge it. As the leader, the fastest way to meet you team where they're at is to use an incredibly short, but very powerful phrase:

"I'm sorry, that was my fault."

In the context of a business, there are always things to improve upon. Your employees want to know that you're trying to actively improve all the time. I began to look for ways in every problematic situation to ask myself where I could have done things better. Not only is it actively taking full responsibility for the actions in your business (which employees are excited to get behind), but it is also a great problem-solving exercise to avoid repeating those situations and making the same mistakes.

Employee was late: "How could I have set better expectations?"

Customer not satisfied: "What decisions did I make that caused this to happen?"

Now, the question that I often get with this topic is:

"If I'm supposed to be vulnerable, what am I supposed to tell them?"

I think the better lens to look at every interaction through while you're working with your team is: "Can I build this relationship right now by building off of what they just said with a relevant personal story?"

If the answer is yes, and it still maintains the professional working relationship, I will be storytelling until I'm blue in the face. We learn through stories best anyway. It's easier to connect a difficult topic together and remember the lesson when it's told through stories. By painting a picture with your story, others can share your experience themselves and imagine it happening to them. So, when it comes to be vulnerable, it's not so much a question of *when* you should spill your guts out, but more of taking advantage of the right timing in the day-to-day operations to open up and expose your human side in small pieces.

If something funny happened, build off it with a funny story.

If something sad happened to an employee, give them a hug and make them feel heard. If you have experience something similar, share. If not, a simple *"I can only imagine what you're feeling right now, how can I support you?"* goes a long way.

There's an old Japanese proverb that says that every human has three separate masks we all wear.

The First Mask is the one that the world sees. It's the one that we put on for strangers, acquaintances, and for people that we have just met.

The Second Mask that we have is for our close friends and our family. It is for our significant others.

The Third Mask that we have is the one that no one sees but us. It is the most private and the most intimate. It is the truest reflection of ourselves.

Employees will start in your business by experiencing your first mask, and some of those relationships will form into friendships that can start to see your second mask, but most will fall somewhere in the middle. Your employees aren't your best friends, but they also should be more than mere acquaintances (although some still might be and that is okay).

Your team will respect you for how open you are to feedback, how much you listen, how much they feel like you get them, and how much you stare at the challenges in front of you and move forward anyway. They respect your scars, your fight, and your grit.

Entrepreneurship is all about "Oh well," not "What if." There's no room for perfect, undented armor in that equation.

Founder Summary

- People want to follow a meaningful vision, a plan to get there, and someone willing to push through challenges; not a perfect record and fancy title.
- I'm sorry, that was my fault."
- Vulnerability is easiest delivered in story form.
- We all have Three Masks: one for the world, one for those closest to us, one just for us.

CHAPTER 10: EXPECTATION SETTING & ASSERTIVENESS

As the leader of your business, you are essentially a professional expectation setter and a professional expectation holder.

Expectation setting is the act of creating healthy boundaries for your team to understand the parameters in which they operate. You might set the expectation that everybody shows up at work ten minutes early. If work starts at 9:00 a.m., that means everyone shows up at 8:50 a.m. at the latest.

Now, it's one thing to set an expectation. Anybody can do that. How will you hold it, though?

If someone shows up at 8:55 a.m., what are you going to do? How you answer that question is a good test for how larger expectations, projects, and the overall working relationships in your team will be handled.

Leadership comes from meaningfully holding tension and holding others accountable to the expectations that you set. You can set all the expectations in the world but if you don't have any follow-through on them, two things are going to happen:

- Employees are going to lose respect for you and you will be viewed as someone they can steamroll over when they're not getting their way.

> • Employees won't achieve the performance they want to see because you're not pushing them forward when they stray off the path needed to get there.

It's really hard to start working relationships acting like a doormat and then swing the pendulum in the opposite direction and become a dictator. Not only will it be shocking for them, but it will break trust.

When you get a new puppy (I'm not comparing your employees to puppies, it's just relatable), it's a lot easier to have the little guy trained on a short leash first so he can get used to your commands, hearing your voice, and navigating the world with that restraint. It becomes part of his comfort zone. Then, when you lengthen the leash later as he grows, the expectations and the lens he has on the world is embedded in his training, and he still behaves on a long leash.

Imagine the opposite. Let that same puppy roam free wherever he wants to go. No restraint and no rules. That same puppy now has a view on the world where he can do whatever he wants. Now try putting a short leash on him. It's going to painfully difficult for you and it will be a crushing transition for our four-legged friend. He's used to having no limits, and now he can only take a few steps. He was used to you being carefree, and now you are yelling at him for doing the same things he did before. It is confusing and upsetting to say the least.

Start with holding the right expectations with your team and then the relationships can flourish and grow strong within them, while getting maximum performance and not breaking trust. To do this, you must have a level of assertiveness. But what does being assertive actually mean?

Assertive behavior is being confident with your decisions without it being "my way or the highway." There is a wide range on the assertiveness scale and where our actions fall on this scale is determined by the direction and intensity of looking after your needs and the needs of others.

On one end, you have passiveness. This is the pushover. This person is agreeable, doesn't stand up for themselves, and constantly bends to the will of others. This is almost always at the sacrifice of their personal agenda. As a leader, nothing is ever going to get done if you're passive, because people will naturally do what they want to do. There's no tension to actions required to hit your goals personally and as a team.

This is person who responds with the *"No big deal,"* or *"It's totally fine,"* when that employee rolls in at 8:55 a.m. It's not doing anything when your new puppy pees on the carpet.

On the far opposite end of passiveness is full-on aggressiveness. Most people often confuse aggressiveness for assertiveness, but they look very different. Aggressiveness is complete inflexibility with others. It is a crack-the-whip mentality that shouts, "Do as I say or you're fired!" At a fundamental level, aggressiveness is leading through fear. It's putting down the 8:55 a.m. employee in front of everyone so you can be seen as the boss that makes the rules.

It was common in older styles of leadership where employees only follow you because of your title. Outside of work though, they have no respect for you. A leader should never be an immovable object. We're talking about leading imperfect humans, not writing a computer program. When you consider the differences between aggressive and passive behaviors, ask yourself this question:

Would your team still follow you if they didn't work for you?

The common confusion that most people have between aggressive behavior and assertive behavior is that they put assertiveness into this box of *"she knows what she wants and won't take no for an answer."* That's simply not accurate.

In all actuality, assertiveness is a happy balance of both passiveness and aggressiveness. On a scale of zero to ten with zero being completely passive and ten being completely aggressive, assertiveness is right in the middle.

Passive	---	Assertive	---	Aggressive

Extreme passive behavior means that a intensely focuses on the needs of others and very rarely focuses on their own needs. Passive people are often spread too thin, drop everything when someone else needs something, and have a tough time getting personal projects across the finish line since their own goals are always on the chopping block when an external request comes.

Extremely aggressive behavior is an intense focus on your needs and seldom on the needs of anyone else. It's me, me, me. Aggressive behavior isn't always yelling and screaming. In fact, it's very rarely that. Looking exclusively after your own needs is mostly done covertly. It's *"how can I get the most out of this situation."* It's *"what's in it for me."* It is setting things up so that you get what you want, regardless of anyone else's satisfaction. It's not listening. Aggressive behavior leaves others behind for personal gain.

Assertiveness is being able to strike a balance between both. It is finding ways to help support others while simultaneously speaking up and making sure that yours are taken care of as well. Since it's a balancing act, it will sometimes feel like a moving target. One situation might call for considering the needs of others slightly more and comprising your needs, while another situation requires your needs to be the main focus.

How does an assertive leader deal with the 8:55 a.m. employee?

That person should be showing up ten minutes early to work, based on the expectations that everyone else follows, but they consistently arrive late. An assertive leader wouldn't let it slip. They would engage the conversation and let the employee know that they missed on an expectation. Assertive leaders wouldn't make a scene and put down the employee in front of the team. They would quietly pull them aside and have a brief discussion:

Assertive Leader: *"Hey, I just wanted to check in with you and see what happened this morning."*

Employee: *"Everything is good, I'm not sure what you mean."*

Assertive Leader: *"Well, we agreed as a team that everyone shows up in the morning ten minutes early and you were later than that today. you're usually on time, what happened?"*

Employee: *"Oh I just hit a bit of traffic."* [you can insert basically any excuse here].

Assertive Leader: *"Gotcha, that's definitely going to happen, thanks for being honest with me. You're a big part of this team, and even if you don't realize it, the team really looks up to you. If you're not showing up on time, what do you think they're thinking? Moving forward, how can I help make sure you're here on time?"*

This is less than a sixty-second conversation, but it lets that employee know that, as an assertive leader, you're paying attention. You are holding productive tension to expectations without breaking trust. Assertive leadership requires listening and understanding without backing down on what was agreed upon.

There is now a very high chance that the employee doesn't show up late again, and on the off chance they are running behind in the future, you're going to get a call or text from them beforehand.

There is an incredible tool and an extremely powerful phrase within that exchange. It is only two words and it works without fail.

"Moving forward…"

Inside of those words are understanding, empathy, respect, and tension to expectations while shifting the conversation from the past and present to the future. The missed expectation cannot be changed now, so dwelling on it doesn't do anyone any good. Shifting the conversation to the future reminds the employee that the control is in their hands. It also reinforces the knowledge that what happened can't happen again without ramifications. It's empowering and not deflating. They are in the driver's seat, and now, every morning, they get to decide what world they walk into: One where they show up on time and everyone is meeting expectations, or one where there are consequences.

When it comes to consequences of any kind, they need to be created ahead of time and clearly communicated and understood. If someone is being punished and they don't know why, or feel like it was uncalled for, it's not on them; it's on you. If someone screwed up, they need to know it first before they get punished for it.

The Three Strike Rule allows constant communication between you and an employee that has missed on expectations, made a misjudgement, or isn't performing up to required levels:

X Strike One: Initial warning. Realigning them to expectations that have been set.

XX Strike Two: A more serious conversation digging into why they have missed the mark repeatedly. This is also when the expectations and the reasons behind them should be thoroughly explained again. Depending on the business, written notice about the situation may be necessary here for documentation. Make it very clear that if the same problem happens again, strike three is most likely termination.

XXX Strike Three: At this point, there have been multiple conversations, and the employee knows their actions aren't in line with the business and your expectations. As a business owner, three incidents are a pattern with this employee and termination is most likely in your best interest, as well as theirs.

All businesses have a range of expectations. From incredibly important to minor infractions, expectations need to reflect your values, goals, and mission. Use your discretion in determining what needs to be enforced strongly and what can simply be a conversation.

With the Three Strike Rule, I found the most success when employees could have the strike disappear after a two-week pay period. It gave them something to work toward while also maintaining clear expectations around the consequences of not following through. I found that after two weeks, if an employee needed to have multiple conversations and meetings to meet team-wide expectations, it was a strong indication for me that it wasn't a good fit.

Using assertive leadership to hold employees to the standards you've established and using the Three Strike Rule can be viewed as the carrot and stick approach.

Before modern transportation, men used mules to pull their carts, and often dangled a carrot in front of the mule and used a stick to slap the back legs to encourage the mule to keep walking. The carrot served as an incentive or reward out in front for the mule to keep moving forward, and the stick created a source of pain at the rear to move away from.

In business, it has been adopted as a metaphor for team performance. When it comes to expectation setting and assertiveness, the three strikes themselves are a consequence and a source of pain for the employee. A reward system, like being able to prove themselves and have the strikes taken off their record, keeps their focus on the control they have for affecting the future.

Founder Summary

- Holding expectations is much more important to building a high performance culture than simply setting expectations.
- Assertive leadership means looking after other people's needs while also looking after your own.
- Remember those two words: Moving Forward.
- The Three Strike Rule to encourage clear communication of consequences and allowing employees to work them off as a reward.

CHAPTER 11: CONFLICT RESOLUTION

The by-product of setting expectations and being assertive is going to be conflict. It's bound to happen. If you're passive leader, you're going to do everything you possibly can to avoid conflict. If you're an aggressive leader, you're going to see conflict as your needs clash with others. Assertive leaders are going to create frameworks to have clear communication to reduce the amount of conflict. But, when it pops up, you need to know how to approach it.

Many people have a negative connotation about conflict resolution and think of conflict as two people butting heads or competing in a screaming match. Although that is technically a type of conflict, there is no basis of resolution in these scenarios of blind anger. The goal of conflict resolution is not sweeping the conflict under the rug, but engaging in it in a healthy way. You want the resolution to still process through the emotion, but then also close it out so both parties can become aligned again and move forward.

Fundamentally, conflict is the friction caused by disagreement. This can happen when expectations are not met, when core values or core needs clash, and when communication isn't clear and assumptions are made. With so many personalities and combinations of needs and preferences, conflict is a fact of life.

This is the foundation that should be laid with your team. Set the expectation that conflict is going to happen and that it is perfectly okay. When they know disagreements are naturally going to come up, and that not everything is going to be lollipops and roses, going through a conflict resolution process is a lot easier and far less emotionally reactive. It's about having the tools to process through the friction versus suppressing it and causing more emotional damage. This will make it feel more like "no big deal" and less "head-exploding catastrophe."

If we have been successful in creating an environment of vulnerability and assertiveness, when problems naturally come up between employees and yourself, they should feel comfortable coming to you about it. They should want to include you in the conversation to process through it and come up with next steps.

If employees don't feel comfortable coming to you about issues before any decisions are made, it means there is a break in trust within the relationship. They may feel like they will be disrespected or dismissed (being aggressive toward them). They might think your opinion doesn't matter (they're already walking over you because of passive leadership). Regardless, opening up to you is uncomfortable.

Conflict is not you versus them. Conflict is you and them versus the misalignment.

One summer, an employee who had just started three weeks before, came to me saying that her family was moving and that her morning commute would take three times as long. She was fitting in really well into the culture and loved her colleagues, but she just felt like she wouldn't be able to make it work. But, instead of just quitting, she came to me with the problem. The environment among the team was open enough where she felt comfortable including me in the discussion, even if it meant her needing to quit.

We were able to talk it through, come up with options, and figure out how we could make it work for her to stick around. She didn't come to me with a decision. She came to me with a problem to help her work through, trusting that I would help her make the best decision for her and the team together. This trust is the bedrock of healthy conflict resolution.

This environment for resolving conflict might be very new for a lot of people working with you, so it's important to remember that there will be growing pains. As the leader, that means you may initially have to be the mediator between employees and help them process through conflict themselves. An environment of respect and understanding is critical here.

There are always two sides to every story, the truth is almost always somewhere in the middle. Allow both people to share their perspectives without interruption.

Active Listening

One person's perspective is not the gospel; it is their interpretation. This includes yourself. You're not automatically correct because you own the business. When conflict comes up, it's equally as important to listen to the other person's perspective as much as share your own. Misalignment is often really miscommunication or misinterpretation.

This can be a tough skill to master, since it's only human to want to be right. The by-product of assuming you are right is that it will lead to a conflict where no one is listening to the other person. We are just waiting for the person to stop talking so we can start making our points again. This is just ammo-loading and it solves nothing.

While they're shooting their word-bullets, your ears are shut off and you are loading up a full clip of your own, waiting for theirs to run out. This only amplifies the feelings that started from the original conflict. It doesn't diffuse them. If we really want to solve conflicts, we need to put down the word-gun and open our ears. This is active listening.

Seek to understand, not to reply...

Active listening is a skill and a muscle. It is the ability to turn off our inner dialogue that is starting to stockpile words and open our ears to just listen. Blank slate. It is absorbing and internalizing what the other person is saying to truly understand where they're coming from. The only way we can truly understand one another, especially during a conflict, is by seeking to understand, not to reply.

The road to empathy begins with this, and it can be very challenging if you've never done it. It's not widely taught in school and it's most likely not something your parents practiced. It makes perfect sense why conflict is a bad word in the eyes of most people. We didn't learn the skills to confidently and productively engage and work through it.

An easy test to determine if you're listening or not is to ask yourself how confidently you would be able to regurgitate exactly what the other person is saying to you. If you can't do that, you're not listening to understand. You're still ammo-loading. When you are actively listening and can repeat back what someone has said, that means that their words have gone from your ears, through your brain circuitry, and have been recreated accurately with your mouth. This process takes 100 percent focus from your brain. No split attention can get this done. Active listening means that the input and the output are the exact same. The words the other person said to you have been spoken back to them like a broken record on repeat.

The other person is going to feel validated knowing that what they're saying is being heard and understood by you. You will have a very clear picture of the differences between your perspective and theirs on the issue causing the conflict.

But how do you communicate your perspective so that they understand? You need to draw a connection between the feelings and the situation. Seeking to understand is a critical starting place, but how can you or the other person understand if what is being communicated isn't clear?

We need to connect actions and emotions. If not, a conflict is just two people endlessly venting with no direction, amplifying frustration, and not resolving the issues. Both individuals within a conflict know the actions or problem that happened because it's external. You can easily see a missed shipment, a defective product, or unacceptable behavior. However, each person only knows the emotion from the situation from his or her own perspective. The only way to bridge the gap and create empathy between both people is to connect the known external actions to the unknown emotional interpretations of the other person.

Did, Said, Think, Feel

"When you **Did** that, it made me **Feel** this…"

"When you **Said** that, it made me **Think** this…"

Using these four words create calm and reasonable ways to communicate your concerns and feelings. Now, the other person knows how you interpreted their actions and you will have clarity on how they interpreted your actions. Often, this leads to a very quick resolution. You are now actively listening and understand the other person. Then, when it's time to reply and share your interpretation and perspective, how do you start?

You ask permission.

After you've repeated back to them what you're hearing and given them the affirmation that you're on the same page, simply say:

"I understand where you're coming from. Is it okay if I share my perspective?"

This technique maintains the open environment for sharing and respects their side of the story. It is really disarming and you may be surprised by a positive shift in their attitude. Since you are asking for their approval, it's not ammo-loading anymore. They have now told you that they are open to hearing what you have to say. This is the key to healthy dialogue. Without permission, it feels like you're stepping on each other's toes, trying to get a word in, and then you are back at square one. It's a powerful concept.

Conflict doesn't need to be bad. It is inevitable in life and especially in business. But, having a common language and the right lenses to view it through will make sure that when conflict arises, it can be dealt with quickly and not leave collateral damage to the relationships. In fact, processing through healthy conflict with respect and empathy will strengthen relationships.

Founder Summary

- Conflict is friction caused by misalignment.
- Your team should be comfortable coming to you to process through conflicts.
- There are always two perspectives to one situation.
- Seek to understand, not to reply.
- Did, Say, Think, Feel
- Get permission to share your perspective.

CHAPTER 12: TEAM-WIDE CULTURE VS. INDIVIDUAL CULTURE

Your team culture is the foundation upon which your whole business is built. A building's foundation is made up of individual bricks, and when they all come together in an aligned way, the strength it can bear is astonishing. Team culture won't be sustainable until we have developed the open communication between everyone like we've already discussed.

But, once that's been established, then performance culture can be broken down into two different forms to be the fuel for an already blazing fire: team-wide culture and individual culture.

Team-wide Culture

When you can combine the personalities of high performers and give them an environment and a common language to communicate, uniting the team under one mission through challenges and reward systems becomes a massive boost to results and connectedness.

Challenges with rewards at the end put the team under productive pressure to come together and achieve something meaningful. The challenge will feel like growing pains and it will test the performance of not only individual team members, but also bond them through a common purpose within the overall context of your goals for the business.

These challenges should not be random. They need to be related to the overall business goals you have laid out. They should also incorporate your team's goals so that it doesn't feel like you are asking for something extra, but is a catalyst to what they are already doing every day.

The motivation behind challenges should be a carrot and not a stick. Most employees will be much more motivated by the pursuit of adding something positive versus avoiding something negative. In our personal lives, this might sometimes be the opposite. In business, if the goal is just not getting fired and keeping your job becomes the reward, negative consequences will deflate positive culture and create animosity instead of productive growth. And even then, if the employee keeps their job, the situation will leave everyone in survival mode. This approach makes team members feel like they have no choice and won't lead to positive engagement or growth.

As humans, we all want to grow and contribute. The culture being created among high performers should reflect this aspect of human nature and not stifle it with stick-style consequences or punishments that need to be done out of obligation.

Positive challenges with the carrot in mind need to be team-wide, and not just for those that cross the defined finish line. Rewards should be given to the team as a whole or not at all. This will it further unite everyone. It will make sure every team member supports each other and that no single employee is left behind. If someone does lag behind, no one gets the reward. The team supports the team. This way, when the team wins and gets the reward, it is a massive victory lap for everyone because they all contributed.

This will often create leaders within the group that champion the importance of the goal and the reward. These people will encourage the people that don't see the full benefit yet and get behind those employees to push them forward. Again, since it's an everyone or no one situation, these leaders go out of their way to help and support others in order to achieve the results needed. Since this positive pressure is coming from their peers (and not the boss), everyone will be more encouraged to pull their own weight so they don't let the team down.

But what should the challenge and the reward be?

It's important that when deciding on the challenge, it is set up to help push toward the goal for the week, month, or quarter. It should be aligned to business growth and very measurable to make it very clear if it has been accomplished or not. Everyone should help decide on the controllable factors and decide what the defined finish line is.

Maybe the goal is to increase the amount of revenue being brought into the business in the next month. If so, you need to have a clear number in mind. The challenge could be to raise the average customer Net Promoter Score from 50 percent to 60 percent in the coming quarter. A challenge could be bringing in a defined number of new leads from marketing in the upcoming week.

It can't be a vague, gray area or a feeling. "Making customers happier" or "working harder" can't be measured objectively or without opinions. There are definitive ways to quantify these types of goals, so pick a metric with a very clear line in the sand. Either the challenge got done in the specific timeline set or it didn't.

You need to be involved in setting the challenge. Whatever it is, this goal needs to be completely aligned to the business. However, when deciding on the reward, it's really important to let the team be in control. You just give the final approval. If it comes from your team, they will be far more excited and therefore likely to hit the challenge outcome.

Maybe it's going out for a fancy dinner if the monthly revenue goal gets hit. Maybe it's taking the team go-karting if the Net Promoter

Score hits 60% or above. Maybe it's $25 gift cards to the company of their choosing if the weekly lead goal is met.

Let them be creative, but make sure the rewards are realistic and appropriate. One thing to also consider when setting these challenges and rewards is groupthink: a premature consensus caused by the urge to fit in.

Come up with enough ideas from everyone to avoid having team members just going with the idea that is being pushed by just one or two people. If the team chooses an option too quickly because they just want to conform or not cause a stir, the buy-in won't be there and the challenge will start on shaky commitment before it gets off the ground.

When choosing a challenge metric and a reward, you need to facilitate the discussion so that everyone is comfortable sharing ideas. That way the challenge fully sinks in and team members are onboard for pushing toward the reward.

Throughout the given timeline for the challenge, your job is to remind the team and constantly lead them to the small tasks that impact the greater outcome. A challenge and reward system for performance culture isn't just *"set it and forget it."* Once it's set in motion, the work begins, and you have to nurture the goal within the team. Like watering a seed, don't expect the team to hit the reward if you don't water it and care for it constantly. Remember, this is still you leading your troops through a battle, regardless of the momentum the business has.

Individual Culture

Within the team dynamic, you will have relationships with each of your employees, and it's critical to nurture them in order to maintain and grow sustainable culture team-wide. The team-wide dynamic depends a lot on the individual dynamics you have between each one of them. When respect and trust exist within the one-on-one environment, respect and trust throughout the team is a natural extension.

Get to know the people on your team. Yes, you know their core needs, their personality type, and their preferences and abilities, but individual culture goes beyond that:

What do they do after work?

What food do they like?

Have they travelled outside the country?

What are their parents and siblings like?

What's on their Recently Added playlist?

Connecting on a deeper level than just colleagues and building a unique rapport with everyone on your team is so important for taking their performance, their growth, and your comfort with them to another level. Vulnerability is easier. Conflict is easier. Pushing their performance and stretching their perspective so they ask more from themselves becomes easier.

When that connection happens, the trust that comes out of it makes doing the challenging things more of a downhill ride versus and uphill battle.

Remember the missed expectations from last chapter? With a genuine personal connection built from that openness and trust, approaching that conversation is a quick tap on the shoulder, not an awkward transaction.

Need to ask someone to do you a favor? Stay late? Help someone else out on the team that is struggling? These conversations become empowering and create leaders based on a deeply connected relationship. They aren't seen as a burden because they work for you and have to say yes to keep their job.

By developing these relationships, employees want to help you and go the extra mile. Even if the title of "boss" was stripped away, they would still follow you based on the relationship.

You need to spend the little in-between moments building meaningful connection and trust while the ongoing momentum of the business continues. This is what separates a team that shows up to meet minimum standards, and a team that repeatedly knocks down brick walls with a smile.

Founder Summary

Challenges and rewards to fuel performance must be:
- Aligned to business goals..
- Positive rewards (carrot, not stick).
- Reward ideas come from the team.
- Avoid groupthink.

Building unique relationships with all your employees:

- Inspiring leadership, getting extra help, and addressing conflict is easier.
- They respect and follow you outside of work.

SECTION 4:
ADAPTABLE LEADERSHIP
& COACHING

CHAPTER 13: GOALS AND PLANNING SESSION: GPS

The easiest way to build consistent performance with you team is by building on individual relationships within focused goal-oriented conversations. This is where having a weekly plan for each one of your employees and a goal to hit creates consistency and alignment with the business.

The best way to execute these conversations is a Goals and Planning Session, or GPS. Just like using GPS navigation to drive to a place you've never been before, this session creates the focused consistency for everyone on the team to regularly review and adjust their actions toward the meaningful goals that they are striving for. The concept of one-on-one coaching for everyone on your team is nothing new, however College Pro developed a framework for setting and reviewing goals that proved undeniably effective for decades. This organization mentored college and university students with no entrepreneurial experience to successfully running five and six figure businesses in the span of eight to ten months. Thousands of times a year, for almost fifty years. This was the jumpstart to my entrepreneurial career and GPS is built from these foundations.

Depending on the number of employees you have, it might make sense to have these sessions bi-weekly instead of weekly. However, more is more with these types of conversations. The more chances you can get to have clear and concise conversations centered around goals, the more likely the goal will be hit. With past employees and entrepreneurs I have coached, I find a weekly GPS lead to the most success.

To maximize the effectiveness of these conversations, they can't be rudderless discussion about goals and challenges. The person needs to have very clear

purposes and even clearer outcomes in order for action items in the coming week to stick.

Each session can be broken down into three parts:

1. Review the past week. How did the results compare to the goal set?

2. Discuss the drivers that caused success and the restrainers that held it back.

3. Make a SMART goal for the next week that maximizes the drivers and eliminates restrainers. (We will dive into SMART goals later in this chapter.)

The GPS is a very powerful tool for setting and hitting goals because of its high intentionality. This framework creates the environment to build deeper relationships with everyone on your team individually, but it also allows you to have much clearer insight into their strengths to help skilfully shape their performance and results in their role.

The point of the GPS is to constantly have a pulse on where someone is in relation to their goals. It is focused time dedicated to having your employees get their heads briefly out of the daily grind and realign to the big picture. It connects the daily grind to the goal. The more you can get a bird's eye view of the forest, the easier it will be to work through the trees on the ground.

For change to happen, the awareness for change needs to be first. A GPS only allows a week to go by before reassessing and resetting if needed. This way, your people don't get so far off course without realizing it and feel like it is impossible to get back on the path and reset.

Review of Last Week

In relation to the goal set the week prior, what are the results? Are the results on pace for the goal? Regardless of the results, it's important as their leader to remain as objective as possible. If the person is behind schedule and the goal wasn't met, he or she will most likely start explaining away the results with stories and excuses for why the goal wasn't achieved.

Don't get caught up in the story. Stories can justify any kind of behavior and performance. Stay focused on the results in front of you as you move into the second step.

Drivers and Restrainers

You need to filter out the stories being tossed your way and look at what happened in the last seven days for the employee to land in the position they are in.

If they are on track or ahead of schedule toward achieving their goal, spend time digging deeper into the driving forces internally and externally that helped them get the results:

How did you do it?

This empowering question puts the responsibility on them in a positive way. It is an action-oriented question that will help you and them define the *controllables*. These are actions that they chose to do, and not things that happened to fall into place.

Did they choose to ask for help when they needed it and save a bunch of time and effort?

Maybe they chose to get up earlier and pack a lunch instead of eating out and they had more energy throughout the day.

Maybe they shifted their attitude and stayed until the work was done and not leaving when they felt tired.

Look for those internal shifts that happened and created good results. These are the opportunities that leaders look for to nurture and support. Doing so will develop further consistency and positive results.

If the goal wasn't hit, the focus on the conversation needs to be on the restrainers. What internal factors served as anchors? What held them back and caused them to miss the weekly target? Again, it's crucial to stay objective here and not get caught up in the excuses and the stories. Believe me. You will hear some stories.

When focusing on restrainers, the more details you can get, the better. You aren't taking on the role of interrogator. This isn't about finding ways to pin the blame on them. Instead, you're searching through the haystack to find the needle: the root problem.

The stories and excuses are a symptom of how the root problem popped up in their week. It's their interpretation of the root problem. If they were aware of the actual root problem, they would gain some self-understanding of the real issue and not focus on the smaller symptoms.

Sorting through the details helps paint a bigger picture and uncovers themes and patterns. They are complaining about the pain and how much it hurts and you're trying to find the pitched nerve that caused it.

If the root problem isn't fixed, goals will continue to go unmet. If you don't process through enough hay, you won't find the needle. The more you can be Sherlock Holmes and dig deep, the quicker you can work through this and come up with options to move forward into the upcoming week and improve results.

When sorting through the root problem after someone misses a goal, understand that it happened for two reasons: skill or commitment. Each has two causes.

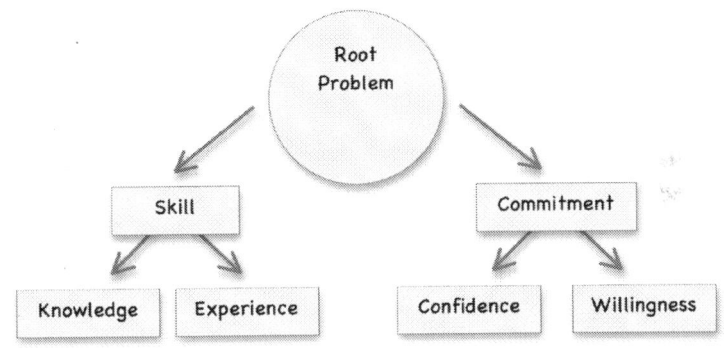

Skill

If the root problem was caused by a lack of skill, it can be sourced down to either a lack of knowledge he has in a specific area, or a lack of experience within that specific area.

They could be so new in a specific field that their ignorance created blind spots they didn't even know they had. Within those blind spots was the knowledge that would have got them to the goal.

If your goal is to ride a bike, but you don't know that your feet need to be on the pedals, riding a bike will be nearly impossible.

On the flip side, they could understand conceptually how to ride a bike, but still has never sat on the seat, held the handlebars, and felt the sensation of speed while the wheels roll under them. This is simply a lack of experience.

There is a difference between knowing the path and walking the path. Any new skill will have a learning curve, and a lack of experience means someone hasn't processed all the way through it to be at a competent level of execution without guidance yet.

Commitment

If the root problem was caused by commitment (or lack thereof), it can be further broken down into either a lack of confidence they has in a specific area, or a lack of willingness in that specific area.

Lack of confidence is generally caused by feelings of not being good enough or comparing their life and abilities to others. Lack of confidence is feeling that success is impossible given the current circumstances. It is often coupled with a lack of experience doing something new and attempting it is in the presence of peers or colleagues. It is fear of judgement. Lack of confidence is feeling like you won't be able to survive outside of your comfort zone, and that is where the task is located.

This person will need an environment with a lot of hand-holding and direction to develop the skill and the be comfortable enough to open up and ask the questions they have without judgement. This will build their confidence in their abilities and their performance.

This guidance is the training wheels on the bike and help holding the seat steady.

Lastly, if the root problem is caused by the lack of willingness, this indicates the team member didn't agree or buy-in on the goal decided on last week. A symptom might be choosing to do tasks that weren't as important or urgent, considering what the goal required. Outside looking in, they might appear to have been straight up lazy.

They might know what to do and have the skill and the confidence to do it, but if the goal doesn't match their strengths and have a connection with personal goals, completing the goal will seem like a transaction or obligation. They aren't fully engaging from a place of inner-responsibility. Lack of willingness is a lack of understanding the full impact that achieving the goal will bring. Lack of willingness is going through the motions without a good enough "why."

In order to get to a place where discussing skill or commitment and details from the week becomes regular, the fundamental element that must happen beforehand is a working relationship built off of trust and respect.

These can be vulnerable conversations, and if you want to fix root problems with your team so they perform better, an open environment during these sessions are critical. If they aren't open to discussing deeper, and more personal skill or commitment issues with you, that's a strong indication that there is a foundational part of the relationship that has either not yet been fully established. This hesitancy could stem from a break in trust or the employee may be new.

The last step in a successful GPS is to take what you've learned about the past week to and make a game plan moving forward into this week that gets them (or keeps them) on track while considering the root problems identified from the week before.

If last week's goal was met, make a clear plan to reinforce what works in order to maintain the momentum. The plan should also include "What Ifs" to consider what back-up plans might be if something doesn't go according to the plan. Help them be proactive.

If last week's goal was not hit, make a clear decision on what has to change. Either the larger goal needs to be reduced, or this week needs to be "catch up." The plan needs to revolve around avoiding root problems or making a step-by-step plan to fix it. This could include more help from you or from the team, additional training, more conversations, or encouragement between now and next week.

The goal itself should be very focused and measurable. SMART goals were introduced to the world of team-management in the November 1981 issue of *Management Review* by George Doran and quickly became the benchmark framework for businesses to create focused goals. However, the version I've found that works best for building up a team using relationships is an adaptation that College Pro used for decades.

Doran's SMART goal acronym is well known as:

Specific, Measurable, Attainable, Realistic, and Time Sensitive.

The adaptation switches out the first S:

Shared
Measurable
Attainable
Realistic
Time-Sensitive

Changing Specific to *Shared* makes each goal a collaboration. You and the employee work together to craft a focused plan for the next seven days that serves their goals and the businesses goals at the same time.

Now there is accountability in both directions. You provide the support necessary to help them solve root problems, and they have someone else watching so they don't get in their own way moving forward. The more people you share your goals with, the more likely it is to happen.

The M stands for Measurable. The goal must have a very defined finish line to make clear if it was met or not by the following week. No rough estimates, feelings, or gray areas here. Did it get done or not? This is the difference between "bringing in five more customers this week" and "bringing in more customers this week."

The A stands for Attainable. Given the current skill and commitment of the person, this goal can be accomplished. The goal should stretch their abilities, but it should still be achievable.

The R is for Realistic. A goal can be shared, highly measurable and fall well within the scope of possibility to achieve. But, can it get done in a week? Does it make sense for the timeline?

Another R that can be considered is Relevant. Does the goal in the next seven days make sense to the larger goals or is it going off in another direction? Ensuring that the weekly goal serves the long-term goals is important so it doesn't split someone's focus. When the short-term and long-term goals line up, a lack of willingness won't be a problem.

The T is Time Sensitive. Having a deadline is critical. Having short-term weekly deadlines is even better. These bite-size milestones are much easier to take action on because it doesn't feel like climbing the whole mountain in a day.

To paraphrase Parkinson's Law, the time a goal takes to complete will expand to the time you give it. If we give ourselves tight timelines, goals don't balloon out of control and get missed. If the timeline is too long, the person may procrastinate, and you will lose productivity.

The other piece of time sensitivity is looking at the objective number of physical hours it will take to hit the goal. This is where the Realistic factor also comes into play. If you set a shared, highly measurable goal that is attainable, but it will take a hundred hours to finish and there are only forty-five hours available, it isn't a SMART goal. The deadline is important, but understanding how much time is required is a necessary consideration for setting yourself and your team up for success.

Lastly, when someone is new to setting goals, they often live in a world of uninformed optimism on the transition curve about what they can realistically achieve in a week. They may overestimate the skill they have and underestimate the time it will take.

Your job is to lead them through setting objectively SMART goals so they build on their skills, maintain commitment, and not be deflated by continually missing goals that were out of reach from the beginning. Soon, they will be more comfortable and confident in goal setting and in their daily work.

Founder Summary

- GPS: Goals and Planning Session
- Don't get caught up in the story.
- Get details to uncover the root problem.
- People miss goals because of either skill or commitment.
- SMART goals need to be Shared goals.

CHAPTER 14: LEADING IN ANY SITUATION

A s the leader of a team, you need to realize that your employees are going to be at different levels of skill and commitment. In order to get the very best performance from them, do not mold them to your style of leadership; adapt your style of leadership to them.

Every skill we acquire in life has a set learning curve. If we are at the beginning stages, we may need everything spelled out for us. Then, as we develop our skills, that instruction becomes suggestions and encouragement. Eventually, our skill set is fully developed to the point where we don't need any hand-holding or support. We look to expand our skill into mastery.

This is the foundation that Ken Blanchard and Paul Hersey laid out in 1969 while writing their book *Management and Organizational Behaivor.* It is now the go-to model for leading people for many of the world's largest companies.

It's called Situational Leadership.

You are recognizing the stages of skill development and adapting your coaching style after recognizing where someone is sitting on the learning curve. As an entrepreneur, this is a critical tool to help your team develop skills more effectively and overcome the challenges that pop up throughout that process.

If someone is highly skilled in an area, you're going to treat them differently in that skill set compared to someone that is brand-new. This may seem obvious to a lot of people, but there are many of leaders that will train everyone in the exact same way, regardless of the variety of abilities and skills within the team. Unfortunately, this cookie-cutter style of leadership has detrimental consequences.

For someone that is brand-new to a skill may feel like they are being thrown into the deep end without learning how to float. Assuming someone has a base knowledge is setting you and them up for failure. It is going to feel like trying to drink out of a fire hose. This mistake won't inspire confidence and may be overwhelming to the point where people will even quit. Too much too soon.

The opposite approach is treating highly skilled people like they're a novice. This type of leadership will make them feel like they're being talked down to like a toddler. It can be interpreted as lack of respect and will break trust. There will be no value established and boredom will happen since they're not being challenged or shown any new perspective. This will also lead to turnover.

The added benefit of having deep, positive relationships with your team is having an accurate sense of what kind of training, leadership, advice, and support someone needs in real time as they develop. This area is not just person-specific but skill-specific as well.

A person may be a master in one area and an absolute beginner in another. There are people that have a PhD in astrophysics but can't cook simple meals. A person may know six languages but can't change a flat tire. No one can know everything, and it is important to realize that everyone has different strengths and weaknesses, as we discussed earlier.

With your team, you will have to be flexible and constantly adjust your style of leadership to best align with their current skill and commitment level. The question is:

There are so many kinds of situations, how do I even begin to figure out how to lead people, not to mention do it on the fly?

Luckily, there are focused criteria that all leadership and coaching scenarios can be divided into. These are four styles based on the amount of direction you give within a skill and the amount of support you give as they learn it:

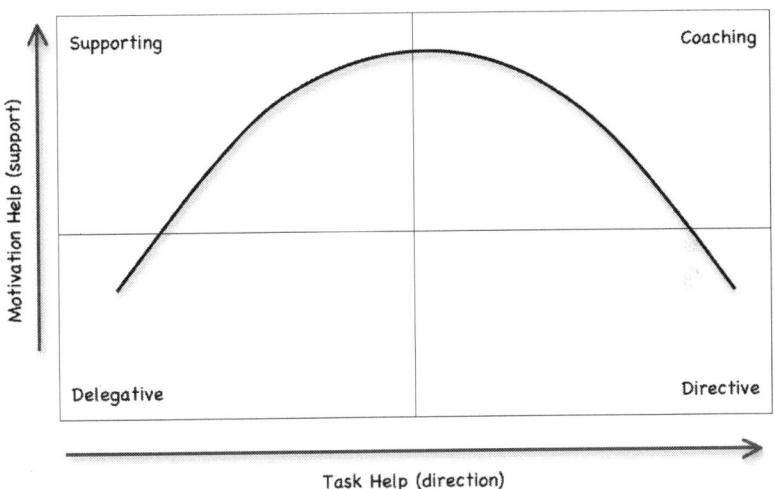

Task Help (direction)

Directive

This style is for people that are just getting started with a new skill. They require technical help learning the skill as they begin to understand the fundamentals. This is almost purely teaching as far as leadership goes. It requires high direction with what to do, what not to do, and frequent communication to ensure that as they make mistakes, you can easily notice and correct them. The learner in this stage is most likely excited to learn and is in the uninformed optimism part of the transition curve. They will be open to your feedback and will quickly implement your directions.

If someone is learning how to ride a bike, a Directive approach would be showing them how to sit, how to hold the handlebars, how to put their feet on the pedals, and demonstrating how all the movements work together by riding in front of them. When they are on the bike, you would adjust their hands and feet so they understand how it feels themselves. As they start to pedal slowly, Directive leadership is holding the seat and instructing the learner to keep their feet moving and to keep looking ahead. All extremely high direction.

Coaching

This is the stage of someone's learning journey where they've developed a base level of knowledge, but have hit their first major roadblocks. Lack of mastery combined with the dip of confidence they are feeling in the transition curve means they need some emotional support as well as direction to help push past the roadblocks they have encountered. This gives them clear guidance and reframes their expectations to give the person a new sense of where they are in the learning curve.

A high Coaching style is needed when they fall off the bike for the first time. They have briefly felt what it's like to have the wheels roll and everything working together, but the lack of skill isn't enough to carry the learner under their own weight without help. Falling off hurts, and it's important to lead them with enough support and encouragement. They can get back on the bike knowing that it probably won't be the last time they fall, but continued learning means they can avoid it.

Supporting

This style is defined by maintaining high support but giving low direction with skill itself. The person has developed enough skill to know what to do without instruction, but their experience with the skill is still low enough that they need help making the right decisions with high encouragement. This is where a coach can help put their experience in perspective.

The learner can now ride their bike with relative ease. The fundamental skill has been established. They aren't falling over anymore, and, with a high degree of confidence, they can pedal, change gears, turn, and stop. However, they still need a lot of help understanding the street signs, who has the right-of-way, hand gestures, and safety. The skill is there, but the high support has switched to understanding how to ride a bike in the real world. These experiences come with their own transition curves. Falling off the bike isn't the concern, but being supported through unforeseen events is important as they take the skill into new environments.

Delegative

This last and final style of leadership. The learner has become skilled enough and has had enough experience under their belt. You don't need to give much direction and direct support. This is self-sufficiency and talent with the skill.

As a leader, the Delegative style is relatively self-explanatory. The leadership you give them feels more like a peer-to-peer relationship. Direction feels more like suggestion and support is more of giving them an ear to bounce ideas off with. They've been there, done that, and now they are doing it in the context of your business.

With our cyclist, they can now go wherever they want with extremely high confidence. They may start pushing their skill by entering a race or go trail riding to grow in different ways. They can ride a bike in their sleep. The skill has now transformed into a hobby or a passion and the person is focused on personal best goals and refining the smallest parts of the skill to feel like they're advancing. This is mastery.

As a leader, we often make the leap from Directive to Delegative too quickly and prematurely think that our team can handle the world. I made that mistake with my painting crew at Tammy's house. As learners or leaders, we always go through all four stages and styles. Some people learn faster, but everyone will go through these four stages to some degree.

Even for high performers, moving too quickly to Delegative will very quickly create a lack of confidence and commitment to a skill. The hard, technical parts of learning a skill must always be combined with the patience to help them navigate the process by building their motivation and experience.

Founder Summary

- Everyone is at different points with various skills: They all require different forms of leadership.
- Directive: High direction, Low Support
- Coaching: High direction, High support
- Supporting: Low direction, High Support
- Delegative: Low Direction, Low Support

CHAPTER 15: HIGH PERFORMANCE LEARNING PLANS

The next stage of advanced coaching and leadership is built off this question:

If I'm supposed to give support and direction for different skills, how do I know what to do?

Good question.

In order to get through all four styles of situational leading with someone in a skill, it is key to remember that no one learns every part of a skill all at once. It happens gradually over time and moving through that time effectively means knowing what to teach when.

With College Pro's mentorship, I discovered that there are four ways to learn something.

- Learned Theory
- Memory Connection
- Controlled Practice
- Real World Experience

Situational leadership is determining where someone is at with a skill and then give them the appropriate direction and support. Depending on their skill level, the framework for a plan to get them highly skilled in that area will be different. It might take two days or two months. The goal now with these learning styles is map out what someone on your team needs and when they need it to get them highly skilled as fast as possible without cutting corners.

This requires thinking back to the needs you have for your business and how beneficial it will be to have that person being highly skilled in an area. The plan also needs to consider how that high skill will also benefit their needs and goals. If it only benefits you, they might not engage in the learning. If it only benefits them, it's not a good use of your time. How does it align to your goals and theirs?

Mastering a new skill usually has a positive impact on your personal and work life. Will those benefits help them hit their big goals? Do they help you reach yours? No trick questions here; the answers need to be yes! If not, that skill isn't important a priority compared to other needs, so help them develop a skill that will benefit both of you.

If they have a specific savings goal and are terrible at managing their money, educating them on basic finances will create clarity on how their paycheck impacts their goals. It can help them see how improving their skills can help them earn more and it will give them a practical skill they can use for the rest of their life.

Learned Theory

This is the abstract knowledge that is foundational to the skill. You can read books or articles. You can listen to lectures or podcasts. You can watch videos. This is understanding a skill at a conceptual or theoretical level without having ever done it before.

This is a pretty common way to be introduce yourself to a new skill and develop an interest in researching the subject. If you want to be proficient, you need to turn this knowledge into practical experience. Learning about something creates the spark that the other styles in this section can support and build on.

If you want to get your driver's license, you'll need to pass the driver's exam. Learned Theory is picking up the latest version of the driver's handbook and learning the rules of the road, the meaning of signs and road markers, who has the right-of-way, how to change lanes, how to handle different weather conditions, and much, much more. You may know these things in theory now, but until you get behind the wheel and use other learning styles with it, you won't become a skilled driver.

Memory Connection

This is where we start to connect the theoretical knowledge back to our previous experiences. It is connecting memories we have that exist around the skill, not directly at it. We may have experienced the skill by watching someone else.

In our driving example, this is connecting the theory you learned from the handbook to the memories you have sitting in the passenger seat. You can learn a lot from watching your parents turn the steering wheel, press on the brakes, and put on their turn signal to merge. This context connects the dots for a learner and makes the abstract theory more relatable.

Controlled Practice

In a controlled environment, you can get your feet wet in trying a skill. Role-playing is a fantastic way to build confidence because the environment is focused and doesn't have the unknown variables that reduce the learner's control to strengthen the skill. This is swimming for the first time with a life jacket on, in the shallow end, with an instructor.

Using our driving example, this is taking the theory from the handbook and what you remember watching others, and then going to an empty parking lot to get behind the wheel. A more experienced friend or family member is in the passenger seat giving you direction as you begin connecting a feeling to what you've learned up to this point.

Since there's nothing to distract you from the task at hand, and there's nothing to hit, you can focus solely on applying what you've learned to start gaining experience. When you make mistakes now, the impact is virtually zero and you can focus on getting it right. You are connecting the theoretical and physical practice of driving.

Real World Experience

This is actually going out there and using the skill. It's where the rubber hits the road. This is where context, theoretical learning, and controlled practice add up to performing the skill out in the wild. Real experience is often the most tangible way to learn new skills.

People need the real time adaptability of a situation to fully cement learning into our brains. All the training up to this point now clicks, and in that "Aha!" moment, the full value of everything that came before is understood. It's fully appreciated and makes more sense. This is often where we realize there is still much to learn, and the cycle can start again.

This is now driving in traffic, not an empty parking lot. You are stopping on red and going on green. Pedestrians cross safely in front of you as you stop and changing lanes becomes second nature. There are a lot of different things going on around you, but since you have had real world experience, you have a much more confident grasp on what to do.

All four methods need to be used to set the learner up for success. High performance of the skill can be achieved quicker because there isn't any wasted time doing redundant things. They are also keen to learn more since the gradual process builds confidence.

When building a learning plan for your team consider the following before deciding to implement:

- How much theory do they have already in the specific skill you're teaching?

- Always Learned Theory first, then Controlled Practice after

- Only transition from Controlled Practice to Real World Experience when they are no longer making fundamental (deal breaker) mistakes. They may not have all the skills (like using cruise control), but those will come in time.

When we get this right, it becomes a massive source of motivation. It fuels the confidence of everyone on the team and the performance culture between them overall. They are getting results, feel supported from you, and are growing as a person.

It's important to communicate to team members that skill development is going to be gradual, but the plan will get them there effectively with all the right tools and knowledge to hit their goals and contribute to your goals as well. That steady building effect will create lasting results.

Founder Summary

- Getting high performance out of a skill takes time to develop
- The learning plan for someone needs to consider all four learning styles:

  - Learned Theory
  - Memory Connection
  - Controlled Practice
  - Real World Experience
  - The learning plan needs to consider if it aligns to your business needs and their individual needs

CHAPTER 16: HIGHER-LEVEL PROBLEM SOLVING

When a team has developed high performance skill and you are mainly using Coaching and Delegative leadership styles, the cherry on top is to give them the ability to solve problems without you and effectively remove yourself as the bottleneck. When the team is empowered and takes responsibility for results, the last thing we want to do is take away the ownership and privilege of solving problems and making decisions.

When the team has the confidence to solve daily problems, they can take more ownership over the work. They feel trusted by their team and you, which creates a lot more job fulfillment. The act of solving problems stretches us and pushes our capacity to be the best version of ourselves. When we open the door for our people to rise up and take on the issues they encounter in stride, work becomes more exciting and dynamic.

This is in contrast to everyone raising their hand to get approval or needing to run something by you before acting. It wastes their time and yours and it creates a structure where all the decision-making weight falls on your shoulders.

You can't be that bottleneck. It isn't in the best interest of your team and your future self. There are two principles that will create a foundation of problem solving. These principles will help arm your team with the tools to solve their own challenges.

- "I intend to…"
- Initial problems and root problems are two different things

I work with the team at Self Publishing School. I noticed that the founder, Chandler Bolt, used the phrase "I intend to…" a lot when bringing up problems at meetings. Why is that a big deal?

It's a paradigm shift for the team because your frame of mind changes once you start adding this phrase on the end of a problem you're facing. Now the problem isn't just the problem. It now has action toward a solution attached to it.

This phrasing and mindset quickly trickled down to the whole team. When someone brought up a problem at a meeting, it wasn't a challenge anymore. It was just information to pass along because they had already thought about multiple solutions.

The brain chemistry shifts to a proactive state when you work within a team culture of solving problems. It becomes an atmosphere of action and resolution instead of constantly asking for help, guidance, and answers. It becomes empowering to not wait on someone else to solve your problems.

Of course, everyone needs input and help with problems from time to time, but when your team has an "I intend to" attitude, problems disappear. You will notice fewer problems because people have the knowledge and power to figure out a solution themselves.

"My computer crashed. I intend to…"

"I am running late. I intend to…"

"I missed my goal last week. I intend to…"

Those three words are the difference between excuses and blame, and between ownership and solutions.

When a problem does arise, we also need to see the difference between the problem being presented and the root problem that caused it. This is the second principle of problem solving.

A lot of entrepreneurs focus too much time on the immediate issue. They want to extinguish the fire. Of course, this needs to happen every now and then in a business, but shifting your perspective and culture to think about root problems will be much more effective for building long term growth.

There is certainly an underlying cause that created the in-your-face problem. Understanding the bigger issues is the difference between sustainable growth and trying to fill a leaky bucket with water. You can add more people, get more customers, and be more profitable, but the pain, and the effort needed from you will still exist. Constantly putting out the little fires is necessary on the surface, but we need to figure out how the fire started. By not addressing the root issues, you will slowly become a full-time firefighter in your business reacting to problems, losing sight of your long-term vision and the growth you want to see in the process.

But how do I know what the root problem is?

When I was consulting for eight-figure companies that had many more moving parts than an average small business, I learned a simple five-step process for determining root causes. For entrepreneurs, it packs a punch and often sheds light on some of the darkest corners of businesses where the largest problems lie. It's called IDROP.

Initial Problem

Data Dissection

Root Problem

Option Generate

Pick and Plan

Since the root problem and the initial problem are two different things, to get from the surface level symptom down to the root cause, we first have to go through the data. Spending time on the data begins to open up our blinders to see the bigger picture by stripping away the emotion of the moment and looking at things more objectively. The root problem is the biggest anchor of all the data. When it is resolved everything else is easier. After identifying it, we can come up with options to eliminate that anchor and finally, take the best option and make a plan of action to get it fixed.

Initial Problem

This is the surface issue that is causing the pain. It could be an angry customer, reduced profitability, or an employee's lack of engagement. Regardless, it's the spark of concern or curiosity that starts this process. If your first instinct it to generate options, it may feel weird and unnatural to pause and not immediately jump into action to put a Band-Aid on the initial problem. Trust me, taking a step back and spending this little bit of extra time is worth it.

Data Dissection

There are two kinds of data to unpack for getting the clearest picture to find the root problem. And it's not only looking at numbers. Root problems are quantitative and qualitative in nature.

This means getting the hard facts, like numbers, but also looking at the emotions and personalities at play: facts and feelings.

The facts you need are everything that affects the initial problem. Numbers, percentages, and stats, and true events that happened within the initial problem are all facts.

The feelings side of data is collecting the perspectives from everyone involved in the initial problem and understanding how it's impacting them. An employee getting yelled at by an angry customer is a fact. The employee's reaction of wanting to quit is a feeling. It's equally important to have both when looking for root problems.

It's important to spend time on data dissection. Root problems are not top of mind, so the facts and feelings that are easily collected off the top of everyone's heads are usually still surface level. There will be positive facts and feelings, as well as negative ones. Be patient and lean in. Give yourself and everyone time to think.

I've been in problem-solving sessions that were two hours long and we spent almost an hour-and-a-half portion collecting and dissecting data. The root problem was discovered in the last twenty minutes of the ninety. Dig deep here. Silence is okay. There are very few times within the day-to-day to have multiple brains focusing on the same topic to fix an issue. Allow space to breathe here. Fixing these root problems will save everyone time, money, and a lot of future pain, so it's absolutely time well spent.

Once the data tank is basically dry, it's time to label all of the bullet points you've made.

Thinking back to GAP sessions you have with you team, label each data point:

> - **High Driver (HD):** very positive and influential; moves everyone forward
> - **Low Driver (LD):** positive, but carries less weight than High Drivers
> - **Low Restrainer (LR):** negative, but doesn't cause long-lasting damage
> - **High Restrainer (HR):** very negative; drains the team; holds back progress

Some factors will be obvious and others may need a conversation among the team to decide it the data point is highly influential or not. Again, spend time sorting through it.

Root Problem

The goal now is to look at your High Restrainers.

- What are the themes?

- Is there one that influences others?

- Are there some that can be combined?

The root problem will often drag multiple things down most often including the initial problem that started the process. What is the High Restrainer that, when eliminated or reduced dramatically, will cause positive ripple effects throughout the team and the business? *That* is the one you're looking for.

Before you look for possible solutions for the root problem, frame all of your options in the form of a question:

How can you eliminate or fix [highest restrainer/theme connecting your highest restrainers]?

Option Generate

Now that we have our root problem, we can now spend time option generating on how best to overcome it. It's important to also spend a meaningful amount of time on this section to exhaust all potential options. What that means is that there is no judgement. All ideas get put on the table regardless of how crazy or unrealistic they may seem on the surface. There's no filter at this stage sifting between good ideas and bad ideas.

When doing this as a team, there are naturally going to be a couple people that will seem to have all the ideas. To avoid groupthink, allow the time and create an open environment, so that all of the ideas are on the table before moving on. Remember when we learned about managing people who aren't like you? You may have team members who are more introverted or don't talk as much, but they could also have incredible solutions.

Pick and Plan

Once all options have been offered, the final step is to pick the most popular one to solve the root problem. There may be a pull to combine all the ideas into one super-solution, but don't fall into that trap. It will become overcomplicated and not get the job done. Stick with one.

The decision-making factors for unpacking this decision of which option is best should be the following:

- Budget
- Timeline
- Team capacity to get it done

Once you have decided on the best plan, pick the people who will address the issue, clarify their roles, and decide on a firm deadline.

You can have the confidence knowing that this work will fix the leaky bucket and solve future problems from coming up. You spent the time and did the work with multiple brains to uncover a very clearly defined underlying problem. Now it's time to get it moving. This process may be new for everyone, so the plan should have check-ins from you to help monitor the progress being made. As the team gets better at this, going through the process will be quicker and require you less and less.

The IDROP problem-solving process may feel cumbersome at first, but as you and the team get more comfortable with the steps and gain a better understanding about what to look for, root problems for surface level issues will start to pop out very quickly, the more this is done. The process encourages sharing, open discussion, and vulnerability, so it will be aligned and an extension to the culture, training, and systems you've already put in place. It will empower everyone to create solutions, and allow you to focus on taking your business to the next level.

Founder Summary

- "I intend to…"
- An initial problem is different than a root problem
- IDROP:
- Initial Problem
- Data Dissection
- Root Problem
- Option Generate
- Pick and Plan
- A team that is confident finding root problems and building solutions creates the foundations for long-term scalability.

Conclusion

At this point you're probably feeling like you have been drinking from a fire hose. So much information, so much to implement, so many gaps and things to be improved. That's okay. Remember where you are on the Transition Curve!

Remember that you won't be changing everything overnight. Rome wasn't built in a day and your business won't have a high performing A-Team tomorrow either. Focus on the process and implement each part step-by-step.

Have "macro patience and micro speed" as Gary Vaynerchuk says. Stay true to your long-term goals while working hard and smart everyday toward them.

My recommendation is that you keep this book with you and always refer back to it. This is a resource and should be implemented from front to back. If you have work to do with your own self-wiring, address that first before anything else. If your first "Uh-oh" moment popped up in building culture and resolving conflict section, don't worry about situational leadership until that is fixed. Stack up these ideas one by one. They are all designed to fit together and be built off one another. Don't do step two before step one.

And take action.

Start implementing today. Nothing changes if nothing changes. The foundations laid out in these pages have created thousands of incredible teams and even more incredible businesses. Your success is on the other side of getting these fundamentals down.

Lastly, if I can be helpful in any other way, don't hesitate to reach out to me: fundamentals@bretthilker.com. I am happy to add value to your world in any way I can.

If this book helped you, your team, or your business in any way, I also encourage you to share it with other entrepreneurs that need it. Let them borrow your copy or gift it to them. We're all in this together.

Going out on your own and chasing down your vision is a hard thing. And hard things need a lot of support. In order for you to win, it doesn't mean someone else has to lose. Let's help all the vision-chasers and world-changers around us by sharing knowledge and learning from each other.

ACKNOWLEDGEMENTS

(Read the last paragraph, it's for YOU!)

I'm so fortunate to have as many support systems as I do, and all of them have played a role in making me the version of myself that I am, and in turn, getting this book to be what it is.

From the bottom of my heart, thank you...

Mom and Dad - For bringing me into this world and raising me to value the importance of working hard for the things you want. Teaching me that are consequences for the decisions you make: emotionally, physically, and financially. For always having my back every time I jumped into the deep end of life. The older I become, the more I am absolutely *astounded* by your unwavering support. Words can't describe how much that means to me. Thank you and I love you.

Krysta - For being the best sister a brother could ask for. I'm so proud of our relationship and the support you've given me. I'm so grateful you decided to be my go-to girl for the business all those years. Your hard work, dedication, and willingness to go to battle everyday, as I figured out this whole entrepreneurship thing, is staggering. Your commitment gave me so much confidence when we needed to push forward.

College Pro - For being the vehicle for the very best real-world MBA anyone could ask for. The support, the people, and the systems forged within your walls have truly dented the world in the most positive way. I will always be proud of the connection I have with you and how you have shaped my life.

Pratik Juta - For your presence. Most of my cherished memories from the past decade have been with you. The parallels of growing our own businesses and teams were a massive part of it, but you and I both know it goes way beyond that. The countless hours plotting our big visions and pondering the universe. The ideas that sparked. And the music; oh the music. The effortless harmony we have and the weight it carries between us isn't lost on me for a second. The future is always more exciting with you. We're going to build big things. For life, my friend. AOH.

Connor Aylwin - For always proving to me that there is more to do. For being an incredible friend and support system when we decided to uproot our lives and move across the country when everyone thought we were crazy. Your focus and work ethic have always been what I measure myself against, and that trip to Portugal was a big part of the reason that this book exists. I always love our reflective conversations talking about what we've grown into and what's coming up next. Let's keep pushing, brother. AOH.

My College Pro Painters Family - For being by far the biggest source of inspiration, growth, support, and guidance for doing hard things at such a young age. Being surrounded by all of you during those formative years as we were all starting our first businesses made the pain of failure feel more bearable, the successes feel more real, and the constant grind all more thrilling. The friendships I forged with you have changed my life. Thank you.

Chandler Bolt - For having the faith in me to add value to SPS. For building an amazing, tight-knit, and supportive A-Team. Your entrepreneurial spirit is a constant inspiration for me to think bigger, innovate, take risks, be proud of failure, and focus relentlessly on growth. I'm honored to be a part of your team and grow with you.

The Self-Publishing School Family - For the endless support as we grow together. The culture of this team is the reason it is impacting the world is such a big way. I love being a part of a team that is as focused on having each other's backs as much as working hard. You have skills and expertise in so many areas; it is truly mind-boggling. A constant inspiration for me. I'm excited for deepening all our relationships.

Jennifer Bradshaw - For making my words sound better than they actually are. My name is on the cover of this book, but it would not have been possible without your feedback and experience to make it the polished version it is now. Thank you dealing with my timeline and always following through. It is truly appreciated.

Cherub and the entire team at 100 Covers - For your incredible work. Many readers wouldn't have picked this book up without your eye. Thanks for dealing with my perfectionism so graciously and working with me to come up with something spectacular.

My Employees - From Tammy's house and beyond, thank you. For the lessons in leadership, relationship building, expectation setting, and conflict shaped me into who I am today. Without your work ethic and commitment to our customers, my businesses would have been nothing.

My Customers - For taking a chance on a young kid with no experience. For sometimes ending up on the short end of the stick as I learned valuable life and business lessons. Your support and trust has been the foundation for the opportunities I've had the privilege to take advantage of.

Danny Kerr - For picking me out of the masses and offering me a completely new path to my life by being an entrepreneur. I sometimes reflect on what I would be doing today had it not been for you and College Pro, and there isn't a version I've come up with that is more exciting. I'm forever grateful.

Leighton Healey - For being a leader and visionary during my formative years as an entrepreneur. Your mentorship and coaching recalibrated my definition of success and allowed me to step into a better version of myself. Thank you for being a role model and believing in me more than I believed in myself.

Zac Johnson - For challenging my thinking when I was thinking too small. For pushing my thinking when it would've been easier to go with the flow. Your coaching took my self-awareness to a new level of clarity. The teams I led afterward were better because of it. Thank you for your wisdom and friendship.

Rodney Larmand - For seeing the untapped potential in me. For always choosing culture over logistics, people over profit, and always going to war for your team. The example you set gave me a benchmark that all my teams will always be measured against. Your support created a home away from home during a high-growth and high-uncertainty point in those early years out East. Thank you so much.

Megan White - For being so easy to work with and learn from. Your willingness to listen, assess, and give me honest feedback made it easy for me to pivot and focus on growth. The way you lean in and take full responsibility is something I have always admired. You work so hard and care so much. Thank you for your friendship and your appreciation of all my puns!

Nick Clement - For being a pillar through the thick and thin of my development while coaching you. Leading a big team and knowing I had you to support my decisions meant the world. Taking the reigns and building something of your own was only logical. I'm proud to call you a friend and to have had the pleasure of coaching you. Full send, brother.

Kelly Stewart - For your love and support during a time when I was constantly being put in front of hard things and even harder decisions. These last few years haven't always been smooth sailing, but among all the other moving parts in my life, you were behind me, no questions asked, even from opposite sides of the country. It is tough to put into words how much that stability, peace of mind, and love helped me. Thank you and I love you.

You! My Readers - For supporting this book and the ideas within it. It was a challenge and a pleasure to write, and the feedback and messages I get make it all worth it. Let's keep connected! I'm happy to add value to your world in any way I can. Thank you!

SPECIAL INVITATION

Send me an email anytime at fundamentals@bretthilker.com if you want to chat!

I get a lot of great questions about the topics in this book and would love you help you so your business can see better results. Don't hesitate to reach out! We're all in this together!

Made in the USA
Columbia, SC
03 February 2020